The First Time

A Memoir of Adolescence

HAMLIN JUNIOR HIGH SCHOOL

The First Time

A Memoir of Adolescence

Kirk Kneeland with Randy Bryson

Breezeways Press

*Since there were so many firsts, everything was so exciting.
Oh, to be that excited about life again*

— Ilene Haugen Wilson

Contents

Author's Note

I am a retired teacher. One day about 20 years ago as I was checking the progress of an in-class writing assignment, a student asked me an interesting question. Michael and his family had just watched the movie *American Graffiti* and he wanted to know if I had been a teenager during that time, the late '50s and early '60s. Repressing a smile, I told him I had. He said, "Boy, you sure were lucky. You had so many things you could do." I laughed and told him that, yes, I did feel I had been very lucky. I'd had a great time during those years. I was in junior high then, and we did do lots of crazy things.

Maybe even a bit crazier was that I spent most of my 32 years in the classroom teaching in a junior high and middle school. Once again, I felt I was very lucky. Here, too, I had a great time.

So it is that I came to write this book. I wrote about what I knew, the world of the adolescent. I scoured microfilm of Springfield and Eugene in local libraries, and relied on classmates' recollections to round out the stories. I am especially grateful to Maureen Mannila for her curiosity, artistic suggestions, and continual encouragement. To Teri McGuire, Curt Dickerson, Glenn Garrett, Ilene Wilson, Janice Sand, and Glenna Johnson for their written notes and support. Also to my brother, Kreg, for his proofreading and suggestions, and to Jennifer Touchette for helping me with the cover and saying "no problem" to all my computer formatting ignorance.

Needless to say, I owe a huge debt of gratitude to Randy Bryson, my partner-in-crime, for his contributions to this book and for his undying enthusiasm. If it weren't for him, I wouldn't be putting this collection of memories together in book form. Using Bob Welch's words, he had the guts to tell me it was time to quit redoing every little thing and "just pull the trigger." The fact that you are reading this must mean that I did.

Finally, I need to thank my wife, Linda, for allowing me the three years I spent plinking away at my laptop writing, revising, and formatting the stories in this book. Luckily she had shelves of books to read and stacks of quilts to distract her. At least I think that's what she was doing.

To the reader: The stories in this book are all things that really happened. Randy and I have told them the way we remember them. It is our truth. Sometimes where we weren't absolutely sure of something, we used our fertile imaginations to connect the dots. Names were changed in most instances to protect the innocent, and the guilty.

As the title says – and like so many things during those years at Hamlin – this memoir is another first for Randy and me.

– *Kirk Kneeland*

Introduction: A Different Time

There's history, and then there's nostalgia. It's been said that nostalgia is history strained through our experiences, hopes, and dreams. Many of our fond memories are enhanced by a yearning for the past, dealing with the insecurity of the present, and a cynical apprehension of the future. Such is this fond remembrance of our years in junior high school.

It was a different time in a much, much different world. It wasn't perfect, nor probably near perfect, but daily living was delightfully less complicated and far from the mantel of to-day's pervasive cynicism. We were naïve but open to the world, wide-eyed and full of curiosity. We blissfully wandered down life's shining path, day to day, unaware of the world-changing issues that were about to impact us all. In many ways, we were protected in the bubble of our small, calm, working class mill town. While the times might not have been as peaceful and bright as we remember, our perspective was untainted by fear, crime, or the untold calamity that was to visit the country in just a few years.

Growing up as a "baby boomer" gave us a life reference limited to the 1950s. We were kids during the resurgent consumer economy and welcome peace that followed a world war and regional military conflict.

First There Was Elementary School

We grew up playing cowboys and Indians without any stigma or shame, certainly without discriminatory intent. For us guys, many summer days and weekend mornings were filled with sandlot baseball, exploring town on our bikes, or playing war. Our heroes were both sports stars we saw in newsreels and World War II soldiers we learned of from our favorite movies. "Normal" was that dads worked and moms stayed home. All my friends had both parents living in the same home. So while I don't remember anyone with divorced parents, I do remember a couple of friends whose mothers worked outside the home. It was different than the norm of the time, but I don't recall any prejudice, positive or negative.

Most of us, after school, during the summer, or on a day off, were assured that if we needed anything, Mom was there. Whether applying a band aid, packing a special lunch, or surprising us with freshly baked cookies, her presence provided a source of serenity and security.

We were puzzled when we heard about racial discrimination because we didn't encounter it. Springfield, Oregon, in the '50s was at least 95% Caucasian, our elementary school 100%. It wasn't something we were proud of. I doubt that we were even aware of that statistic. It wasn't something we thought about. Some kids used racial references, stereotyping certain groups of people with names they must have heard ("Eeny, meeny, miney, moe, catch a ...") from their family. We sometimes naively repeated those names without any understanding of the true meaning or the amount of hurt they could inflict. If we did repeat those words most of our parents taught us, sometimes with unpleasant consequences, that certain words and phrases hurt others and were not to be spoken.

Families felt safe in their homes, neighborhoods, and our town. Many times we would be gone on our bikes all day, visiting friends, playing sports, and exploring our city from end to end. Many days, Mom would make us a sack lunch to take with us and not expect us until dinnertime. We had to be home for dinner, but afterwards we usually went back outside to play until the ringing of our silent evening alarm clock when the streetlights came on.

On a whim, we could come and go at our own house or stop at any friend's home. There seemed to always be someone ready to give us a cold glass of Kool Aid and a snack. No one wore a bike helmet (they didn't exist) or carried a cell phone (there weren't any) and adults seemed to not worry about us. None of us locked our bikes. There was no need. Our parents knew that if we encountered any trouble, we could knock on almost anyone's door and have them call home for us. Because in a small town most people knew each other, it was also common knowledge that any missteps would get back to our parents. When someone told someone else that told another person, the communication string would eventually include someone that knew our moms or dads. Because we never knew who was watching, we did the right thing (most of the time).

If we thought of it, our family might lock the front door at night, but if not, it seemed no big deal. Many people left the family car unlocked, some even with the keys in the ignition, a contributor to what we later learned were joy rides.

Police were respected and trusted. It never occurred to us to question the authority of police, school officials, or any parent-aged adult. We might joke around with each other, but those I knew never showed disrespect directly to adults. In short, we were secure in the warm cocoon of our town. Bad things happened to other people in places far away. The TV nightly news was benign, focusing on natural disasters, local events, and, to us, totally boring politics. There might have been an occasional criminal story, but it was reported without the sensationalism now expected and ninety-nine times out of a hundred, it had occurred in a place remote from us. In most cases, our parents protected us from disturbing news of any local crime or negativity. It was adult stuff and they kept it that way.

School taught us the basics of reading, writing, arithmetic, history, science, and penmanship. Respect was demanded and discipline expected. Disrespect such as talking back to a teacher was not tolerated. The last thing we wanted to experience was the storied and dreaded trip to the principal's office.

In elementary school, discussion of social issues and current events were usually limited to the Weekly Reader, a newspaper for students we looked forward to receiving every Friday. It was from that newspaper that we learned such critically important information as how to pronounce the name of the French Prime Minister "Sharals DuhGahl." Social responsibility came in the form of scout troops for boys and girls, band/choir concerts, and traditional pageants. Our school mornings always began with the Pledge of Allegiance, standing tall beside our desks. We had bake sales, fundraisers, and we were instilled at an early age with the idea of personal charity.

Churches were important, no matter the faith or denomination. We may have attended different churches than our friends, but that didn't divide us. Even those who didn't regularly attend church services participated in church-based food or clothes drives, social events, and charities. Each faith sponsored families and individuals that might need assistance, held soup kitchens, or gathered donations to help those less fortunate. Everyone seemed to be okay with religion in what ever form a person chose.

We were very fortunate to have the opportunity to experience the value of honest work at an early age. A good part of our summers were spent in the bean fields, strawberry patches, or cherry orchards. We learned quickly that if we showed up everyday and worked the harvest, we would make enough money to buy school clothes for the following school year. These life lessons began for many of us in elementary school, instilling a solid work ethic and fostering a realization of basic personal economics.

As kids, we were aware of some adults that drank too much and some relatives that got "lit" on Saturday night. There were uncles, aunts, other family members, or neighbors whose behavior embarrassed us when they drank alcohol. No other drugs existed in our world. Our personal exposure to alcohol consumption circled around legendary rumors of dropping an aspirin in a Coke or adding some of Mom's vanilla extract to a soda because it had alcohol in it. A busy social event might bring an opportunity to sneak a sip of someone's drink when they weren't looking, but if it happened, it happened. Memory doesn't recall it being that important at our early age.

We went to the local theatres to see double-feature movies, a newsreel, coming attractions, and a cartoon or two. Our parents didn't worry about us being introduced to objectionable, violent, or sexual content. Movies had built in standards. More importantly, society had standards. Some nights our parents piled a group of kids into the family car and went to the local drive-in movie.

We remember radio shows, like *The Lone Ranger*, *The Shadow*, and the kids' favorite, *Big Jon and Sparky*. However, the golden days of radio were being displaced with a new media in front of our eyes. Television came along in the early '50s, black and white and fuzzy. Either there was a tall antenna on the roof, or "rabbit ears" on top of the television set, sometimes enhanced with tin foil and inventive placement. Not everyone had a TV, sometimes neighbors hosted other families for certain favorite shows. Broadcast hours were limited. Before coming on the air in the morning and after hours at night, moving images were replaced with a familiar test pattern featuring an Indian in full headdress.

There was censorship in movies and television, but the vast majority of standards were more attributable to a sense of civility and limitations. It seemed that most people didn't test societal limits just because they felt entitled to do so. Instead, self-restraint was expected.

Then There Was Junior High School

Our junior high years, 1958 to 1961, were also an era of innocence, peace, and respect. Our focus was on learning social dynamics, forming bonds, and experiencing the relationship challenges that would serve us the rest of our lives. We took every day in stride, but most importantly, we were allowed to be kids and grow up at a reasonable, leisurely pace. Information available to us was age-appropriate and we were not put in adult situations or forced into adult choices.

Little did we know that we were on the cusp of a radical societal transformation. We were clueless that the next decade would include seeing three national leaders, including a president, assassinated. We had no idea that a small country in Asia would become the focus of a major military action, nor that many of our friends would fight and some would die there. The looming violent turmoil that would lead to fulfillment of the promise of civil rights equality wasn't even a thought for us.

It is from our recollections about those years that these stories have come. A special force must have been at work to reunite us (Kirk and me) and rekindle our collective memory. By utilizing what's left of that memory, we found a common understanding of the uniqueness of those days and offer these stories, our stories.

Most importantly, these are memories we fondly present of our years at Hamlin Junior High School in Springfield, Oregon. We remember the first time we encountered many of life's challenges and the decisions we made. Unexplored before, these were our initial adventures into adulthood, from social flubs to questionable decisions and unimagined consequences.

To our contemporaries that attended junior high during or near to these years, we welcome you back to that special time. For those that weren't there, please enjoy our reflections, candid thoughts, and the unintended humor of that very different time.

After all, it was our first time.

— Randy Bryson

The Green Hornet's Midnight Ride

Unlike the rest of us, Earl "The Deviant" Dwyer began practicing for his adolescent rebellion while still in elementary school. During October of his 6th grade year Dwyer's parents left him with his grandparents while they headed to eastern Oregon for a few days of deer hunting. When his grandparents went to bed that Friday night about 10, he slipped out the back door to collect a few of his friends – in his folks' 1953 Chevy. His parents' and grandparents' houses were only a block apart.

The first stop on his midnight ride was at the Mill Street gym where he collected Willie McAllister and Jerry Hollens, two of his Moffitt classmates.

"Are you sure you can drive this thing?" asked Jerry.

"Well, I got this far didn't I? Just get your butts in." Once they had shut the doors Earl continued.

"Look, my dad lets me back this car around all the time. He even lets me drive our little jeep along the dirt roads when they go to sight their rifles in at McGowan Creek," said Dwyer. "Anymore more questions?" With that he headed for his next pickup at the little grocery store on 7th behind the high school. When he pulled up a few minutes later, two girls piled in the back seat with Jerry. Willie hopped in at shotgun next to Earl.

"Hi guys," said Tonya, trying to keep her giddiness bottled up inside her slim 5'8" frame. Her sidekick that night, Jessica Stone, smiled and waved as she plopped down on the other side of Jerry.

"Where we going?" asked Tonya.

"Oh, I just thought we'd take a little ride. See what we can see," Earl replied.

"Well, Earl, buddy, if you get tired or feel this is just too much for you, I'd be happy to take over," said Willie.

"How you gonna do that, Willie?" asked Jerry. "You'd need three pillows under you even to see over the steering wheel and Earl would have to push the pedals while you're trying to steer."

"Oh funny, Hollens. At least I'd have both my hands on the wheel," shot back McCallister glaring at Hollens then smiling at Jessica.

"Let's go, Earl," urged Tonya. The Deviant dropped the column shift into first and they motored north into the night. When the Chevy reached K Street Dwyer turned right and headed east past the Northgate Market on the left and Risher's on the right. At 14th Street Earl came to a stop and waited patiently for the light to turn green. When it changed he turned left and proceeded along Mohawk Boulevard then followed the curve to the right and onto Mohawk-Marcola Road. Trying not to attract any attention Earl cruised easily past the Springfield Airport then hung a quick left onto 29th. About three blocks later he turned right onto Industrial and abruptly stopped the car.

"OK, Willie, you wanted to drive. Here's your chance. Slide over and sit in my lap. I'll work the pedals. You steer," said Dwyer. "I think it's time for you to pilot the Green Hornet." Little Willie, all five feet and 83 pounds of him crawled onto Earl's lap and grabbed the wheel. Tonya reached over the seat and placed her hands over Willie's eyes.

"Gee, Willie, I'd like to drive, too. So would Jerry and Jessica. How about if we all pitch in and drive the Green Hornet like a team. It'll be fun. Earl'll work the pedals, you grab the wheel and steer, and Jerry will be your eyes. I'll try to keep you steady."

"What about Jessica?" moaned Willie.

"She'll do her best to relax you while you're driving," smiled Tonya, "so you won't feel like this is too much for you." Tonya nodded to Jessica who settled herself on Jerry's lap and leaned over the front seat. Earl revved the engine a couple times then dropped the gearshift into low.

"Here we go, Willie." He eased out the clutch and the Green Hornet began to roll.

"Tell me how I'm doing. Do I need to turn? When? Left or right?" shouted a frantic Willie. Just then Willie felt another pair of hands – on his neck.

"You just need to relax, Willie," said Jessica. Her hands gently rubbed his ears then slid down and massaged his shoulders. "You're doing fine."

Jerry directed Willie through two gentle curves at low speed then Earl pressed down on the accelerator, shifted into second and increased the speed to a screaming 10 m.p.h. Willie blanched.

"We're into the homestretch, Willie boy," he said.

"God, don't let me crash, Jerry. JERRY?" Just then a close-by mill whistle blasted.

"Look out for that train!" screamed Jerry. Earl shoved in the clutch and slammed on the brakes. Willie ripped Tonya's hands off his eyes. The green Chevy sat straddling a railroad spur line. Willie looked everywhere but didn't see any train.

"You stupid bastards," yelled Willie. The four other passengers began to laugh. Willie slid off Earl's lap and to the far side of the front seat. He turned his back to the four great pretenders and stared out the window.

"Oh, cheer up Willie," consoled Tonya. "You were such a good sport – and driver – I'll buy you a Coke when we get back to town." With Willie clammed up refusing to acknowledge the others' existence, Earl took over. The late night ride continued down Industrial to Commercial and then right onto 42nd Street. The Green Hornet soon nosed up to Main Street. Earl turned right again and headed back toward town.

"Be on the look out for cars, any cars, either coming up behind us or coming towards us on the other side of the road. Some of the mills like Roseboro are changing shifts right about now. Seeing a bunch of kids out at this hour cruising may draw their attention. It sure would if one of those cars was a cop making his nightly rounds."

Sure enough, about a mile further down Main Street as they were approaching Leather's Oil Jerry yanked his arm from around Jessica's shoulder and shouted, "Cops." All four passengers dropped to the floor below window level. The muffled giggling and wriggling pile of bodies on the back seat floorboard drew Willie's ire.

"Shut up, you idiots," he said. Glancing to his right Earl eyes registered the black and white police cruiser tucked up behind a distant gas pump. Gradually reducing his speed he slid right on by.

"Good eyes, Jerry. I think he was just waiting to nab a Roseboro worker or two laying patches on their way home." At 10th

Street the light turned red. Dwyer stopped. The Green Hornet idled easily. All the passengers remained huddled on the floor. The light turned green and Earl shifted through the gears and into third. "You can come back up now. The street's empty," said Earl. Jessica, Jerry, Tonya, and Willie eased back up onto the seats. "Let's see if Hull's is still open," said Tonya. "I owe Willie that Coke."

"Not much chance of that. This place looks like a ghost town," said Jessica. "And look, all the lights are off in Hull's. Looks like no Coke for Willie tonight." Sensing a bit of disappointment and realizing the trip was nearing an end, Earl looked down the normally busy street and then in his rearview mirror. Darkness everywhere. No movement. A silent switch flipped in the Deviant's mind. Earl slammed on the brakes right in front of the McKenzie Theater.

"Chinese fire drill. Everybody out." All four doors sprang open and five yelling bodies raced counter-clockwise around the green sedan then piled back and in and slammed the Chevy's doors. Earl, smiling, shifted through the gears easily and headed the remaining blocks to Mill Street for a right turn. While the others, impressed with their bravado, laughed and chattered nonstop, Earl's eyes scanned the darkness.

"Well guys, this party is coming to an end. I'm going to drop you off where I picked you up and let you make it back to your houses on your own. Time for me to take the Green Hornet home and let the old fella rest." With that Earl dropped first Jerry and Willie and then Jessica and Tonya off at their respective stops and then eased the green Chevy sedan into his empty garage on West N Street. The short walk to the back door of his grandparent's house offered no excitement or surprises. That was just fine with him. The "midnight ride" had, like Paul Revere's, just made its own 6th grade history.

The New Brokers of Cool
(A Wofford Fantasy)

My first day at Hamlin Junior High was a study in extremes. Here I was, the normally cool Bruce Wofford, beyond excitement entering the seventh grade, ready for a daily schedule that featured seven class periods, six different teachers, personal lockers, and "really neat" older kids. I was on an adrenaline high in anticipation of how "cool" it was going to be to be a junior high guy – hopefully a popular one at that.

Just three months earlier at Moffitt Grade School we had, as sixth graders, been the top of the heap sixth graders. We felt we ran the school. Not only were we the oldest, but we had exclusive rights to be the brokers of what was "in" or fashionable. We ruled the school and set the standards, or so we thought. As guys we cruised the halls making radical fashion statements all with the collars on our white shirts turned up and our hair slicked back with Wildroot Cream Oil. In short, we were way too cool for school and we knew it. Moving ahead to junior high would mean we inherited the chance to be even bigger trend-setters, as if that was possible.

So, on that first Monday at Hamlin, we were poised to march confidently into the new world of seventh, eighth, and ninth graders, secure in our cutting-edge fashions as we defined them. We were so full of ourselves that our naïve cocky blindness blocked recognition of what we were about to encounter.

Little did we realize that we actually faced the daunting task of rising from the very bottom of a much more sophisticated social order. Our elite group figured that we would stroll in on that first morning with the same sense of entitlement that we had casually flaunted the previous school year.

We were so clueless. We had no idea that being cool now had expanded context and more complex rules. It was an exciting new experience, with elements both good and bad, much like plunging into the deep end of the pool before you really knew how to swim. Within those first few days, our giddy and exuberant confidence was to be shattered and replaced with the very real, palpable fear of the seasoned eighth and ninth graders.

That first day I was haunted by long stares from older boys standing in groups. They glanced at us 7th graders and then moved on to derisive sneers, taunting laughter, and open mockery. Groups of 8th and 9th grade girls were also gathered in giggling bands, but they seemed so caught up in their drama that seventh grade boys weren't even noticed. On that first day, just being a seventh grader turned out to be challenge enough. Then a poor fashion decision on my part turned the day into one of my recurring adolescent nightmares.

Earlier in that summer of 1958 I vacationed with my parents in Oklahoma and Texas visiting relatives I had never met.

It was our first airline experience. It took two days to get to Oklahoma City. We stayed overnight in Denver. It was also my first night in a hotel with more than one story and our first encounter with a rental car. When we finally reached our destination the feeling of complete culture shock and regional disorientation overwhelmed me.

Oklahoma was a strange foreign land, introducing me to a society far outside my experience. The extended family I met was very different from anyone in Oregon. It seemed like every sentence had at least one *y'all* in it, and it took me awhile to get used to people *fixin'* to do things. Hobbies revolved around *huntin', fishin', runnin' the hounds*, as did the favorite pastime, *sittin'* and *whittlin'*. Hours were spent *visitin'* on expansive front porches drinking from bucket-sized glasses that held what I thought must be five gallons of sweet ice tea. Watermelons were grown on the farms, and it was a commonplace treat to just *bust open* a melon and eat the sweet middle, or heart, discarding the rest.

The local drawl forced me to seek translation on occasion and at times my blank stare told my parents I was struggling to interpret unknown terms and phrases. At other times, when parents weren't around, I nodded politely and sometimes I had no idea what was said. It was also a summer where new cousins tutored me in the graphic facts of life phrased in unique ways never entertained by my ears. Apparently, growing up on the farm had huge advantages when it came to sex education because they knew lots of stuff I had no clue about. *And they were not afraid to tell me everything they knew, whether it made sense or not.*

One day, I visited a small, local department store in Maud, my parents' hometown. While walking down a narrow aisle in the General Store, a unique pair of pants caught my eye. These pants were definitely not something I had ever seen in Oregon, and hadn't yet been judged by my friends as to their fashion appropriateness. *What could they not like? I prayed they came in my size.*

Growing up and shopping in a small Oregon town meant that we all bought clothes at the same places. We all wore the same styles and didn't have the opportunity to be radically different. Teen fashion and fads emanated from southern California for the most part, but we kept it conservative and followed what others wore. This pair of pants was so different, however, that I was sure they might initiate a new trend. *Where did Oklahoma get such fashion, I wondered.*

Checking with my slightly older cousin, he assured me that the style, material, and color of these pants qualified as the height of adolescent fashion.

"Y'all will be sumthin' in them pants", my Oklahoma cousin drawled.

"Are you sure?" I asked him. "I've never seen anything like them in Oregon."

"Y'all wait till people see em'. Them is finer than frog hair," he boasted.

By this time, his validation and assurance had rocketed my imagination to adolescent nirvana. I knew I had to have them. They were so totally different than anything in our town. They weren't like the common jeans, cords, or khakis at our schools. I was sure that these pants were meant to draw attention and cause everyone at Hamlin Junior High School to marvel. *Instant popularity.*

"Are you sure you'd wear those to school?" Mom asked, offering some initial resistance and confusing skepticism.

"Mom, they would be my favorite pants and I'd wear them every week," I assured her. She agreed to purchase them for me, but her reluctance puzzled me. What was the problem? *They're for junior high school. After all, what do adults know about cool?*

From that moment, I swore to myself that those pants were to be the crowning feature of my wardrobe for my first day in junior high school. I pictured myself with friends, new and old, clustering around me, marveling at these exotic pants, as I sauntered down the hall between classes or leaned against my new locker.

Summer seemed to drag after we returned from our trip. It took forever for August to pass.

September finally rolled around, and on the night before school started, I lay awake creating scenarios of how popular these pants were going to make me. *Did you see Bruce? He has amazing pants, so unique, so cool!*

On that warm September morning of my long awaited 7th grade year, I jumped out of bed at first light, got scrubbed, brushed, and combed, and slid into my new pants. I felt elated. Nothing like this had ever been seen in Springfield, Oregon. *Wow, these are even greater than I remembered I thought as I slipped them on.*

Rather than catching the usual school bus, Mom drove me that first morning. On the way, my eyes caught hers several times as she glanced down at my pants. It seemed that she wanted to say something, but just smiled and wished me a good first day. I jumped out of the car.

Up the sidewalk I strutted with confident anticipation, already noticing people alerting others to look at me. I turned into a breezeway and headed for the area of the school where my home classroom was located. My eyes flashed down to check my pants and I once again marveled at how unique they were.

Ahead of me, at the entrance to the 7th grade wing, a group of five or six upper classmen forming a circle in front of the double-doors. They were all uniformed in jeans, white t-shirts, and blousy blue coats, which I would later learn were called bomber jackets. As I approached this gathering of obvious friends, I heard laughter and verbal jousting coming from them and I anticipated that their attention was about to be focused on me. Here I go. *This is going to be so great. I'll probably be one of them by this afternoon.*

To enter the hallway, I had no choice but to penetrate this circle of ninth graders, but was safe in the confidence that my pants would impress them and grant me amnesty for my intrusion. After all, they were smiling, laughing, and having a good time. *And just wait to see what happens when they get a load of these new pants*

This was to be the first in a long series of poor decisions regarding social hierarchy that highlighted those early days of my seventh grade year.

Confidently penetrating that social circle and approaching the equator, my ears perked up to hear the anticipated "oohs" and "ahhs" as they noticed my new pants. After what seemed like a long silence, instead of hearing amazement, it began.

Snickers became laughter. Then laughter became raucous laughter followed by a cacophony of catcalls.

"What a farmer!"

"Did you get those from a special ed kid?"

"Watch out for bulls."

"Is this a joke?" There were more comments, but my attention was directed to getting out of there as soon as possible.

The continuing rash of comments put me unceremoniously on notice that rather than rating the pants as ultimately cool, my fashion sense had apparently violated some unwritten, hidden, sacred adolescent code. After the initial shock, I realized the cruelty stemmed from a sudden realization that we were now the lowest common denominator in a highly skeptical and cruel social pecking order. Cool pants seemed to not be the answer. In fact, I was getting the feeling that they were not perceived as cool. *How could this be? What happened to the scene I had previewed for a couple months?*

Apparently, vividly bright and shiny slick fire-engine-red pants with thin black pinstripes were outside the boundaries of cool in this new society. They were different – bright and noticeable – and completely unique. My confusion coupled with the sudden realization of the situation eventually turned to anxiety and dread. *How could they miss the special statement these pants make? Don't they see how I stand out in a crowd?*

The jeers and taunts deteriorated into laughter and cruel name-calling for what seemed like hours rather than less than a minute. I couldn't find a convenient hole to crawl into, so I jerked open the door and quickly wove my way through the crowded hallway to my first period class where I silently slithered into a desk at the back of the room. As I glanced around, classmates were whispering and looking in my direction, some chuckling and pointing. I prayed quietly for everything from my waist down to disappear, or maybe that all of me could just be invisible for the rest of the day? *Would it be worse if I just took them off? After all, maybe people would notice my underwear less?*

I navigated the rest of the day by walking in larger groups and hiding behind people as much as possible. My friends and I found many ways to avoid the eighth and ninth grade boys, which proved to be useful for the many weeks and months that followed. I tried to understand how I had missed the boat so badly and digest the fact that there were new brokers that determined fads and fashion.

I also had yet to clear my confusion about what wasn't cool about my pants. I mean they had a little gold buckle in the back and a very thin plastic chrome belt. What wasn't to like? Well, some people must not have been able to deal with how unique they were, but for whatever reason, the message was clear, something about them missed the cool designation. My friends avoided commenting about my pants. They stayed quiet about the subject, just avoiding judgment and distancing me.

Moving covertly in the student herd to the school bus that afternoon, I was relieved when I slid into the seat near the back of the bus. There were no upper class boys around. Finally, this day had reached a merciful end.

I jogged quickly from the bus stop, darted in my house, bounded up my stairs, and made sure those pants were well hidden in my closet. That's where they stayed until we gave them away a year later.

Those pants were worn and judged only that one time, but on that infamous day I learned my first lesson in social acceptance. It became a guideline, maybe a rule, for life. To assure that you are "cool," always be aware of who is in charge of that designation.

Anticipation

Anticipation's always greater than the real thing I remember Dad telling me. But the September day in 1959 that I boarded the school bus for my first day as an 8th grader in junior high, I was sure he was wrong. Butterflies were having a field day inside my rib cage. I was riding away from Saint Aloysius school uniforms, catechisms, nuns, and lunch boxes. I was headed toward a collection of new teachers and classrooms, PE showers, my own hall locker, and more than 200 new eighth grade classmates. Seated across from me on the bus was Dave Gillette, my next door neighbor and the current student body president of my new school.

"How ya feelin', Perdue?" he chuckled knowing that I was wound tighter than the rubber band on a balsa glider.

"OK," I replied, amazed that I was already out of breath after just two syllables. Dee Howell, a perky 13-year-old who had spent many a summer morning in the bean field telling me about what Hamlin Jr. High would be like, waved to me from two seats back. She'd said she'd introduce me to her group of friends. Dave said he'd help me with all the stuff I needed to do to get onto the 8th grade football team. Luckily, I wasn't going to go into all of this by myself. In my hands I clutched a school map and copy of my class schedule. My brother, Scott, had spent the previous year as a 9th grader at Hamlin and had explained how to get to my classes. What had seemed clear last night, however, all seemed incredibly murky now.

The bus pulled up to the unloading area. Chattering and joking, kids piled out. No sooner had my feet hit the sidewalk than a loud buzzer sounded. I realized I had only a few minutes before first period began. Dee caught up with me as I stood staring at the school map in my hands.

"Lost already, I see," she laughed. "Come on. I'll show you to your first class. It's right next to my P.E. class." She tugged on the sleeve of my coat and I followed her down the breezeway. After two lefts and a right I found myself standing with a mob of kids outside a locked classroom door.

"See ya later," Dee said and bounded off for the girls' dressing room. Quickly scanning the group I realized I was, indeed, on the outside looking in. I knew no one. A few minutes passed and then the door opened. Everyone ducked in and found a seat. The teacher cleared her throat.

"Good morning, class. My name is Miss Sloan. You are in period one and this is Arts and Crafts. The first thing I am going to do is take roll to make sure everyone is in the right place." I had grabbed a seat near the middle of the class. To my right sat a lanky freckle-face boy named Rick and to my left a muscular swarthy boy with slicked- back black hair in a DA who said his name was Jordy. They seemed to be friends and joked back and forth as Miss Sloan began calling names.

"Steven Archer...Kristy Baxter... Ritchie Edwards..." Kids either raised their hands, said "Present" or "Here" and Miss Sloan continued down the roll. I awaited my turn. "Mark Perdue." Without thinking I jumped to my feet. "Here," I said. Six years of parochial school training died hard. I was frozen in the teacher's stare. My classmates turned to gawk at the new kid.

"You may sit down," said Miss Sloan. Red-faced, I dropped into my chair and immediately began looking for a hole to crawl into. I kept a low profile and somehow survived the rest of the period. When the bell rang I was one of the first out the door.

I made it to an empty desk in second period Algebra quickly and watched the other kids filter in. Annette Jensen, a tall, slender brunette with a bouncing ponytail slid into a seat two rows over. When Jeff Merkel, the boy across the aisle from her, made some comment about her freckle count she swung a lightning-fast right that smacked him on the shoulder. Later I noticed him rubbing it several times during class. Mary Alice Monihan was the last in. She squeezed in at the last second, her conversation to the boys in the hall snipped off as Mr. Renwick closed the door. She headed to the far corner of the class. All the boys eyes and smiles ushered Mary Alice to her seat. When Mr. Renwick began calling roll I gripped my chair so I wouldn't repeat my first period humiliation.

Third period science with Mr. Barrow was a distinct change of teacher personalities and appearance. Instead of the close-cropped and receding brown hair of the lanky Mr. Renwick, I dropped into a middle-of-the-class seat to see a short, snappy dresser in white shirt, tie, and spit-shined shoes. His slicked-

back auburn hair and drill sergeant demeanor brought back
the law and order feeling of my former St. Al's nuns. Breaking
into a grin for recognizing a familiar atmosphere, I began scanning my new classmates. To my delight Dee came bouncing in
and sat right in front of me. Other familiar faces followed: Jenny Harris, a pleasant girl on my bus, and Marcy Mellum, a girl
I recognized from the youth group at church. Ronnie Trumbo,
a 13-going-on-21 eye-popper took a seat just across the aisle to
my right.

The last kids in the door were three guys, shirttails out,
hair greased back in DAs. They headed to the back of the classroom. Tracy, the heavyset one with the black leather jacket and
silver spike ring dropped his notebook loudly on his desk and
plopped down. RJ Black and Farley Sanderson announced their
arrival in similar fashion. As I secured myself for roll call once
again, my peripheral vision detected Ronnie sneaking looks at
me. When I turned her way she snapped back to the paperwork
Mr. Barrow was having us complete. Using my suave demean-
or, I began playing the same game. The time in science flew and
before I knew it the bell rang. I let the other kids in the class get
up and head towards the door. Even though Mr. Barrow hadn't
assigned any homework, I had given myself some: Ronnie.

With that assignment on my mind, I completely lost track
of 4th period. I snapped out of this pleasant reverie when the
4th period bell rang signaling the end of morning classes. I
hurried to my locker, dumped my books in, and grabbed my
lunch bag. Following the throng I easily found the cafeteria.
As I entered Dave waved me over to the table where he was
sitting. He introduced me to some of his friends and invited me
to sit down. I ate my sack lunch and answered the occasional

question thrown my way. Most of the time I sat in awe of the number of kids in the cafeteria. Even if I discounted the 7th and 9th graders, I now had almost 10 times the number of 8th grade girls to look at as I'd had in the entire St. Al's 7th grade.

It didn't take me long to get the system down and learn the rules. After a couple of weeks I had made a few friends in each of my classes and gotten onto the football team, which gave me additional connections. Instead of being on the outside of that circle I encountered on Day 1, I sensed myself moving ever so slowly toward the center of things. In the center were the athletes, the class clowns, the female divas – the social trend setters. That was where I wanted to be. I just had to find a way to get there.

MR. SAUL T. ROSE, PRINCIPAL

Instructors at the Asylum

After lunch time, I finished the day with Soc. Studies, P.E., and Language Arts., two heavies and one light class. That first schedule featured three remarkable teachers from my two years in junior high. The fourth teacher I learned about one day after football on the activity bus.

Gus and His Guillotine

In algebra that 8th grade year I had a wonderful, though slightly eccentric teacher, Mr. Renwick. The grapevine had it that for years kids had referred to him as "Gus." The name seemed to fit. He was tall, slow-speaking, and incredibly logical. Although just in his early thirties, his short hair was already receding. Teaching junior high will do that to a person. He had a big bass voice and could generate the most comical expressions because of his rubberized facial contortions. He was sort of like Joe E. Brown teaching math.

MR. RENWICK

The second day in Algebra I got a definitive clue as to what kind of a person I would be dealing with. Mr. Renwick opened the small closet at the right front corner of the room to deposit his lunch pail. Hanging from the center coat hook in that closet was five-foot white cardboard skeleton. An index card with the word "MOM" in large black capital letters was stapled to the skull. This was my first hint that "Gus" might not be your run-of-the-mill teacher.

Mr. Renwick definitely had some distinctive quirks. For instance, if a student was not paying attention in class and tried to fake it by giving an off-the-wall answer to one of his probing questions, Mr. Renwick would fix his upturned hands on his face in a kamikaze mask and bellow "Nnnnrrrowww," imitating the sound of a World War II dive bomber. Then he'd move on to someone else and ask the same question.

If you were dumb enough to be so loud or disruptive that others couldn't learn he might jettison his normally calm demeanor entirely. The offending person(s) would be called to the front then turned to face the class. He would have them do "lighthouse." This meant they were required to turn around slowly five times while repeatedly sticking out their tongue(s) and blinking their eyes. Then they returned to their seat(s) – and paid attention.

He also had a unique Renwick-style twist to a common classroom situation, throwing things into the wastebasket. At the end of the class period students typically threw away scratch paper or old assignments they no longer wanted to keep. There were always those, of course, who dreamt of being future NBA stars and wanted to see if they could wad up their papers and hit the trash can from their seat in the classroom. If they made their shot, they were heroes and cheered by their classmates. If they missed, Mr. Renwick dumped the whole waste basket out and they had to stay after class and pick it all up. On a warm afternoon about three weeks into the school year I was witness to a bizarre execution. A large wasp made the mistake of flying through an open window into his classroom uninvited causing a bit of mild panic. Mr. Renwick stopped teaching. He grabbed a newspaper – he always had a stack in class – rolled it up, and silently stalked the winged intruder. When he got close enough he swatted it gently to stun it. Then he slid a 3x5 card under the paralyzed creature and brought it to his desk at the front of class. On his desk sat a mini guillotine about six inches high. He placed the insect on the block and slowly – for effect – raised the blade. On cue the class did a finger drum roll, and the blade plunged downward beheading the unfortunate insect. He swept it off into the trash can and resumed his teaching as if nothing had happened.

J.C. and His Friend "George"

My PE teacher, Mr. Johnson, was another student favorite. He was young, handsome, and athletic, all the things adolescents idolize. He was also a consistent disciplinarian. During the '50s and '60s corporal punishment was allowed in schools, and the most visible tool of enforcement for male teachers who chose to use it was the hack paddle. Mr. Johnson had one crafted especially for him by some masochistic 9th grade boys in shop class. It was laminated mahogany about 2 1/2 feet long with 1/2" holes drilled in the wide part of the paddle. He named it "George" and kept it in his office in a red velvet-lined violin case.

Students who got to know George intimately were kids who got into fights in P.E class or broke the rules. Offenses that brought hacks were things like swearing, wearing unstenciled or stolen P.E. gear, snapping someone with a towel in the dressing room, or throwing soap in the showers.

MR. JOHNSON

And J.C. – Mr. Johnson's real first name – loved to make the offenders sweat. For example, let's take the infamous stencil check. Every day at the beginning of class you'd hear the "on your numbers" command. Every student in class had been assigned a number which was marked in paint along the sideline of the basketball court for the purpose of taking roll. Every once in a while J.C. would begin the roll routine with the words "stencil check." Kids were always forewarned that this was going to happen because J.C. would write it on the locker room chalkboard. That is unless Butch Cluff, the sadistic PE helper, erased the notice. He did that a number of times.

Mr. Johnson was just performing a routine check to make sure everyone had the same shoes, socks, jocks, shorts, and shirts that they had stenciled with their initials during the first week of school. Anyone wearing anything that was not theirs had to step out of line. J.C. would send Butch to get "George" while he recited the rule about wearing only your own clothes and not "borrowing" things that didn't belong to you. Meanwhile all the non-offenders in line were, like Butch, secretly salivating for justice to be exacted. When Mr. Johnson was handed the paddle he would walk up and the guilty student would bend over and grab his ankles. Now for the fun. J.C. would practice his paddle swing for the whole class to see much like a golfer does before he/she is about to smack the ball. Lots of practice swings. Meanwhile, the student had to wait. And wait. Then came the swat. Never given in anger. Never hard. The hacks were all just quick wrist snaps that embarrassed the offender(s) in front of their peers and maintained a sense of order. The hacks that might have been the most dreaded were the ones given to dripping wet shower offenders. I saw the red stinging imprint of George on a few damp rear ends during my two years at Hamlin.

The last thing that I associate with Mr. Johnson was what happened to guys that got into a fight anywhere else in school. The principal let them resolve their fist fights at lunch in the large gym. Mr. Johnson, as PE teacher, was assigned to be the referee. Each of the boys was given a pair of gigantic boxing gloves to wear. They were allotted a maximum of three rounds to fight, each round lasting two minutes. I never saw any boy get hurt in the slightest and I never saw any fight even get to the third round. The fight was over whenever the boys got so tired of throwing those huge gloves at each other that one quit. If one boy had enough at any time during the fight, it was over. And, at the end of their fight, they were required to shake hands.

Panties and Prostitutes

Ms. Enns, my young language arts teacher in 9th grade, didn't need to rely on guillotines or hack paddles. She had her own style of intimidation. A theater major by training, she wore her long brown hair in a ponytail and sported tortoise shell horned-rimmed glasses. Nothing about her struck me as fluid. She was staccato, stiletto, and dramatic. One day Emily, a pert, raven-haired socialite, tipped her chair back a few degrees beyond the balance point and crashed noisily to the tile floor. Her full pink skirt flew up over her head giving everyone a brief but full view of her underwear. Scrambling back to her uprighted chair, Emily covered her red face in embarrassment. "I see you at least wore a matching outfit today, Miss Vinson," remarked Ms. Enns. The class giggled.

MS. ENNS

Another afternoon a couple months later the class was taking turns reading sections of a short story out loud. Open textbook in hand, Ms. Enns strode back and forth across the front of the room. Other than the student reading, the only detectable sound was the rhythmic click of Ms. Enns' heels as they struck the tile floor like the sound of an amplified metronome.

Then a loud "POP" shattered the classroom rhythm. Instantly Ms. Enns spun 90 degrees to her left and glared at the class.

"Only prostitutes pop their gum," she blurted, her verbal machine gun blast spraying the class. The girls were aghast at her words. The guys seemed to perk up at the word "prostitute, " but I don't think we really got it. Shock effect seemed to be one of her favorite weapons.

By contrast, one day Ms. Enns brought in a record of classical/jazz selections and asked us to write down the color we associated with each band of the LP. I thoroughly enjoyed that exercise and think from that day on I looked at writing in relationship to the other arts in a completely different way. Music, colors, art somehow were now connected in my head to the stories I was reading. Leave it to this theatrical lady, bizarre as she was at times, to flip a critical switch in my understanding of how things might go together.

About ten years later during a summer college class entitled Poetry and Photography I put together a slide show presentation of Joni Mitchell's song "Both Sides Now." I remember thinking of music, color, and art again. I don't know if Ms. Enns would have been smiling if she had known. Probably smirking would be more like it.

Knowing No Limits

Mr. Nielson, a science teacher, every so often had a flair for the dramatic. His students loved it.

"A couple of days ago in Mr. Nielson's science class he did something that really blew us away," said Delmar Dykes, our gangly left tackle. "Almost literally." He laughed. "He was demonstrating the fact that pure sodium metal reacts with water. He cut off a small sliver of sodium in the storage container (sodium is stored in oil so it does not react with the moisture in the air) and put it in his water

MR. NIELSON

dish at the front of the room. It skittered around the water's surface giving off a few small sparks and a little water vapor that looked like smoke. We, of course, loved the demo and urged him on, wanting to see what happened when he used more. He then cut a larger sliver of sodium and the reaction in the dish of water was a little more violent. The class was again thrilled and we clamored for more. This continued until the sodium blew up in his face and left a mark on the ceiling of the classroom. When sodium reacts with water lots of heat and light are given off. The heat ignites the hydrogen and you have a nice hydrogen explosion."

After graduating from high school Delmar worked for the school district delivering supplies to the schools. He was happy to see the ceiling scars from the explosion still remained in the old science classroom.

Looking at these teachers after having spent years in the classroom myself, I can see the importance of what I learned, even though I didn't know I was learning it at the time.

From Mr. Johnson: being fair and consistent in disciplining children, whether I was raising them or teaching them, and never attempting to discipline when angry.

To Mr. Renwick: a person could invite others to learn through the use of humor and unusual props.

And from Ms. Enns: eccentricity has its place – different types of teachers work for different types of students.

As for Mr. Nielson: a ceiling attests to the fun in pushing the limits to entice kids to learn. As Mark Twain once said, "I never let my schooling interfere with my education." For me that might have been more accurate than I knew.

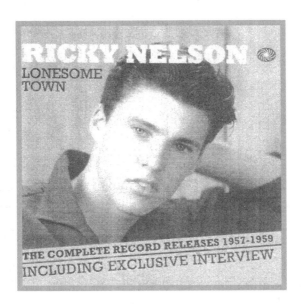

Spaghetti Dancing

Transitioning from a small private elementary school to a huge public junior high in 1959 had its pluses and minuses. I was definitely interested in all the pluses: athletic opportunities, academic offerings, and way more students. Instead of the 40 students in my combined 7th and 8th grade class at St. Aloysius, more than 500 kids jammed the Hamlin cafeteria at lunch. And unlike my St. Al's class, at least half of those 500 wore blouses and skirts.

Besides all these benefits, a source of fascination for me was the dance the school allowed each day during the last 15-20 minutes of lunch at the far end of the cafeteria. Most of the "popular" kids were there, either dancing or trying to. It was on the fast dances that the diminutive Jimmy Beltron and socialite Jenny Juliano really shined. Even more curious to me, though, was the dynamic that came into play during the slow dances. It was during these that it was socially acceptable for a boy to put his arms around a girl and a girl to reciprocate. At these noon dances there was no nun loudly clearing her throat or any chaperones racing around trying to slide textbooks between two dancing bodies.

When a guy got up enough courage to walk the 30 feet across the floor to ask a girl to dance one of the slow dances, a primitive form of the "box" step usually ensued. That's if she was lucky. Most of the guys I watched were much more comfortable spinning slowly in a tight circle as if their right foot had been nailed to the floor.

"They don't seem to be too interested in showing their dance moves," I overheard Jackie Mulder, a rally girl, tell her small circle of girlfriends. She rolled her blue eyes and chuckled. "Other things seem to be occupying their minds."

What I soon realized was that no matter what the guy thought, everything after the couple clasped hands and turned to face each on the dance floor seemed to be controlled by the girl. She could be like a bundle of spaghetti, either cooked or uncooked. Her choice. And the placement of her right hand made her choice perfectly clear.

One September afternoon Butch Cluff, the cocky fireplug who played right guard on our football team, decided to test the waters and zeroed in on his target.

"I'm going to give Annette the chance of a lifetime," he said rubbing his hands together, a nervous laugh betraying his confident claim. He waggled his eyebrows, flashed us all a lusty grin, then beelined across the floor. When he reached the tall brunette tomboy, I saw her smile and nod. They headed into the rush of couples in the center of the floor. Santo and Johnny's *Sleepwalk* began to play. Butch encircled Annette's waist with his left arm and began his slow python-like squeeze. The laughter and polite conversation ceased. Annette stiffened and pressed the heel of her right hand just below Butch's shoulder blade. No compliant spaghetti for Butch on this dance. Question asked. Answer sent. All in less than three minutes.

This same scene I watched reenacted every lunch period. Sometimes, though, a girl's answer was what every hormone-ravaged 13-year-old boy dreamed about. Her hand would go the lucky boy's neck or shoulder, and he would happily extinguish the daylight between their two bodies.

It was during one of these noontime dances that I received my first-ever invitation to that adolescent male dream. That was the day I finally asked Ronnie Trumbo, the 13-going-on-21 flirt in my science class for a slow dance. I was just being friendly. Fortunately she accepted.

Everything started innocently enough, but about 63 seconds into *Lonesome Town* – some things you just don't forget – Ronnie's left hand slid up on top of my shoulder. The barrier had been lifted. Now what was I going to do? Nervously I pulled her closer. Wasn't that what a guy was supposed to do? I had anticipated this happening some day with someone of the opposite sex, but the day hadn't been penciled in on my social calendar. As we turned slowly during the song my eyes locked on a group of my football buddies clustered at the edge of the dance floor. They were smiling at me and whispering to one another. I caught them waving at other guys across the dance floor and pointing to me, grins erupting on their faces.

The dance ended. We separated and Ronnie's brown eyes rolled up to lock on mine. She smiled. I smiled back. We exchanged "thank yous" then turned and walked back to our respective support groups. A couple more dances and the lunch period ended. As the cafeteria emptied and we headed to our lockers to collect our books for the next class, I glanced to my right and saw Ronnie's group of friends engaged in frenzied conversation. They all turned and looked in my direction. Ronnie flashed a quick smile then hurried down the breezeway.

That afternoon while getting dressed for football practice, Earl "The Deviant" Dwyer and Bruce Wofford, my best friends, kidded me about what had happened at lunch.

"Whoa, Mark. You like Ronnie?" Bruce teased.

"I don't know," I said. "It's not like I planned that to happen, you know."

"Yeah, right," Earl laughed. "You telling me you didn't enjoy what every guy who looks at Ronnie dreams of?" I just waved him off and replayed the scene in my head. It had been kind of fun. So this was what it was all about. All the locker room conversations, the bragging and boasting and jokes. Obviously, there was a reason the nuns at St. Al's hadn't held lunch time dances. I was just beginning to understand why.

The next day I was introduced to yet another level of social intercourse, written notes. As I entered my first period Arts and Crafts class, a girl I didn't know thrust a neatly folded paper triangle about 1/4 inch thick into my hand.

"Here, this is from Jenny," she said and then raced away. It took me a while to figure out how to unfold the note, but once I had I quickly read the short message. *Do you like Ronnie? She thinks you're cute! Write me back. Jenny.*

What was I getting myself into? I needed help. I needed to talk to The Deviant and Bruce, but in the meantime I wrote back. *Jenny, I think Ronnie's nice. She's fun to talk to. Mark.* I was trying to be tactful and was at the same time thrilled that a tantalizing girl thought I was cute. I folded my note up in a small rectangle and passed it to Jenny when I saw her in the hall.

The note passing from Earl and Bruce and me to Ronnie and Jenny and their friends continued for the rest of that week and into the next. So did the noon dances. I danced with lots of girls and also with Ronnie, of course. I would meet her a couple of times during the day and walk her to class. Thursday of the next week Bruce handed me a note from Ronnie. It said: *Mark, I REALLY like you. Meet me Friday after school by Room 7. Love, Ronnie.* Love? My hands grew moist and my throat tightened. I started searching for Bruce.

Bruce only lived a couple blocks from school. He said he'd go with me if I wanted. Friday arrived just as it normally would have, no matter how much I wanted the week to reverse course and have it be Wednesday. I was looking both forward to Friday after school and dreading Friday after school. For an adolescent Catholic boy, it was about the same as the pre and post-confessional scenario. By the time the last period ended on Friday I was resigned to my fate. Bruce found me and we walked, in an extremely roundabout fashion, to the enclosed breezeway area of the Arts and Crafts room. As we turned the last corner and approached our destination I froze. About 20 feet away Ronnie and Jenny stood in the alcove just in front of the door to room 7. About ten feet away from them were four of Ronnie's girlfriends. Bruce and I got nearer. Jenny left Ronnie and joined the group of four. Bruce stopped.

"Go see what she wants. I'll wait for you here." I walked over to where Ronnie stood tucked away from view in the small alcove.

"Hi," I said. "You wanted to see me?"

"Yes," said Ronnie in a soft voice. "We've been sort of going together for the last couple of weeks. "I think you should show me that you like me. I want you to kiss me."

The group of girls had either heard Ronnie or knew this was what she was going to say. Clutching their arms to themselves they swallowed a shriek.

Kiss? My first real kiss and it had to be on stage in front of a group? I wanted to talk about the weather. What I was doing this weekend. How much homework I had. But to kiss her right here, right now, in front of all these people? I had been taught how to read, how to add, subtract, multiply and divide, how to diagram sentences. I had never had any instruction in how to kiss a girl. And now it was put up or shut up time. I looked into Ronnie's eyes, then stepped forward with my right foot, grabbed both her shoulders and pecked her on the lips. Without uttering a word, I turned to escape, smacked my left knee on the edge of the brick alcove and limped to where Bruce waited.

"Let's go," I hissed through clenched teeth, then hobbled as fast as I could in exactly the opposite direction of Room 7. Somewhere in my adolescent fantasies I know I had anticipated kissing a girl. I just didn't recall my fantasy being anything quite like this.

The following Monday I kept a fairly low profile hoping to avoid Ronnie and just blot that previous Friday trauma from my life. I made it through period 2 but then entered Mr. Barrow's science class for 3rd period. Ronnie glanced at me and then down at her desk as I made my way to my seat. I felt myself curl up and retract like a pill bug that's just been touched.

When the bell rang for lunch I rocketed out of the room to my locker. I hurried to the cafeteria, my lunch sack in my hand, and settled into the safety of my guy friends. I said little, just ate my lunch in the comfort of the circled wagon of buddies. I could sense, though, the questioning glances of Ronnie and her friends. They wanted to know why the sudden abandonment on my part. I wanted to disappear.

That evening on the phone Bruce asked me the question I had been dreading. "So what are you going to do about it?"

"I guess I'll have to talk to her, but I'd just rather evaporate and go to Mars for a few weeks," I said. The next day I handed Bruce a note to give to Jenny to give to Ronnie. I wanted to keep hold of my ten foot pole.

"I'm too chicken," I said. "Will you help me with this, Bruce? I want her to know I like her as a friend, but that's all I want it to be. Nothing so serious." In truth, I wanted to be friends with all the girls, not tied to one.

The morning drug by like trying to run the 100 yard dash waist deep in the swimming pool. Science class was sheer torture, but somehow I again made it to the sanctuary of the cafeteria. Then 15 minutes later, just as I was finishing my peanut butter sandwich, my eyes caught a blur of colors in the breezeway outside the wall of cafeteria windows. Ronnie was in the center. She looked up and through the windows right at me then burst into tears. Ronnie and the blur that encircled her raced off around the corner. *Oh, God, smooth move, Perdue. Now you've done it. Aren't you proud of yourself.* This was definitely not the way any fantasy I'd ever had was supposed to play out. But it had. I had just received my welcome to the world of adolescent romance.

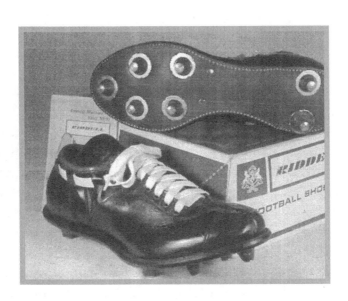

Ah, Shoe...T

O ne of the saving graces for most boys of early adolescence is the P.E. class. It is a place where their boundless energy gets a chance to be released in activities and games. Even if you were genetically wired to be a klutz, at least you got a chance to exercise muscles other than your eyelids. The more coordinated boys usually chose to exercise beyond the regular P.E. class in one after-school sport or another. Some were even involved all year long. Such was my situation.

It was Friday, my first period class that very first week of school at Hamlin. The morning announcements rolled out of the PA box high on the south wall. Hot lunch menu, various club meetings, and then one that drew my attention: "All boys wishing to participate in flag or tackle football meet in the Boy's Gym at 12:15 today."

I made it through morning classes. In the cafeteria I quickly tossed down my peanut butter sandwich and half pint of milk then followed the throng of guys headed to the Boys' Gym. Saul T. Rose, the well-worn principal, introduced the coaches. Mr. Buss was responsible for the 7th grade team, Mr. Carlile the 8th graders, and Mr. Johnson the 9th graders. The principal wished all the teams good luck then left the gym. Mr. Johnson covered all the information and requirements.

"Everyone will need to get a physical and purchase a jock strap." Mr. Johnson paused, looked up at the 9th graders, and flashed a sly grin. He continued. "Eighth and ninth graders will also need to buy a set of football cleats. Everything else will be provided."

While the 7th graders got to play flag football and could use their PE gear and tennis shoes, the 8th and 9th graders got to engage in their testosterone-charged favorite, big boy tackle football just like the Ducks and Beavers, the Chicago Bears, Green Bay Packers, and San Francisco 49ers.

A week after our initial meeting, practices began. In our crowded locker room 34 guys tugged on pants, helmets, and pads, laced up their cleats and clicked across the cement floor to the grass fields beyond. Regrettably, I looked nothing like the bruising NFL backs or sleek receivers I watched on TV at home on the weekends. A big part of it had to do with my shoes. Fully dressed I looked like a white fire hydrant with lumberjack caulks.

Dad had bought me my first cleats; they were black high tops. No self-respecting ace running back wore high tops. Those were for the low-geared bulldozing linemen. Lusting after the low tops that the Baltimore Colt's Raymond Berry wore – black Ridell oxfords trimmed with a white-laced collar – I folded down the top three inches of my boots.

I couldn't fault Coach Carlile for not calling my number much that 8th grade season. I felt like an oversized tortoise, not a cheetah. No way I could be elusive and speedy with those black high tops weighing me down. When I was handed the ball and got tackled, I wanted to wind up on the bottom of the pile, my clodhoppers hidden from view. Every adolescent jock knows instinctively how critical it is to feel sleek and look good. At least I got a white plastic helmet, not one of the black leather ones that a few on my team got. All of the helmets, regardless of the material, sported a single bar face mask. One 9th grade linebacker, however, chose a white helmet that had no face mask. His name was Ricky Reilly. He loved to growl and grunt at the running backs, and after his tackles, spit gobs of dirt and grass. It was just a primitive form of intimidation; he wanted us all to recognize how really tough and manly he was.

On the field and in the locker room I tried to stay clear of those cocky 9th graders, especially the twin Neanderthals, Lonnie Poole and Lenny Krasselnick. Both of these knuckle-draggers were well over six feet tall and daily ate their quota of nails and blackberry vines for lunch. Zits and hair covered their backs and faces. Even with my cleats and helmet on, I barely came up to their armpits.

We, as 8th graders, were content to let the 9th graders beat each other up. We had our own challenges. The first was learning how to give Bruce Ott, our stud running back, the ball 40 times a game. The other was how to use trickery and deception while our opponents were focused on stopping Ott. That meant that occasionally Jungle Jim Turanski, our Patton-tank fullback, got a hand off up the middle, Jerry Hollens, our quarterback got to throw a pass, or Tommy Johnson or I got to run a sweep or reverse. The sum total of that year's four-game schedule resulted in 2 wins, 1 loss, and 1 tie. The 9th graders, despite their size, lost all their games. We kept real quiet that season in the locker room.

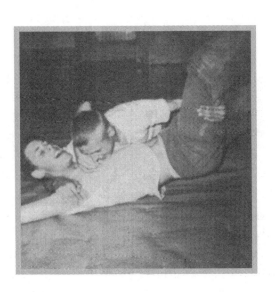

The Mat Rat

When football season was over, it was over. This was a time when a player could put away the football cleats for a whole year and not get them out till late summer of the following year. There wasn't the expectation that you would automatically engage in a weight room program, begin a winter league, or join a traveling team. No sport was a year round commitment.

You were never asked to specialize in only one sport. You were encouraged to try them all. Players enjoyed the respective sports seasons because they knew they would be over all too soon and that would be it for the whole year. So it was that in November I handed in my football gear and looked forward to basketball starting in six weeks. That and a little down time.

It was then that one of Sister Martha Mary's famous little phrases reared its ugly head: "Idle hands are the devil's workshop." I was up for a devilish bit of idle time, but my football coach and soon-to-be basketball coach, Mr. Carlile, had a different plan for me. In fact, he must have had a quick chat with my favorite nun.

"You really need to stay in shape, Mark," he said to me one day. "I want you to turn out for wrestling. That'll be a great activity for those of you who want to enter basketball season in good condition."

I was deflated and a bit nervous. I'd never wrestled anyone other than my brother, and that I did only in self-defense. I had no desire to roll around on the mat with another guy rubbing our sweaty bodies together and smelling each other's armpits as we grappled on mats every afternoon. But I did just that and emerged a month later learning how to apply an arm bar, perform an escape, and complete a single or double leg takedown.

My favorite escape turned out to be from the district tournament where I managed to flop around enough to grab a third place. I wasn't a champion. Ron Wilkes, a wiry little second string running back and about 30 pounds lighter, could tie me in knots in under a minute if he really wanted to. I was a humble survivor.

I prayed no one I knew would ever show up to one of our matches. I was just marking time and trying to stay in Coach Carlile's good graces. I'd never played any team sport that didn't have a ball, and I didn't plan to make a habit of it now.

Earl Offers a Prayer

After my wrestling servitude, basketball season began. I was back in my comfort zone again. As an elementary student at St. Aloysius, I had played in the Goldenball tournaments in Mac Court on the University of Oregon campus. And even before the official 8th grade season began I was registered in the official Hamlin basketball record books. The previous year, my last at St. Al's, we had played the 7th grade Hamlin team. I was named the St. Al captain for that game. My soon-to-be good Hamlin buddy, Earl Dwyer, playing for Hamlin, had rebounded one of my team's errant shots and, in a moment of confusion, banked the rebound into our team's basket. He was mortified on such a large stage to have done this, and as captain, I was officially credited with his two-point effort. Thus, I was already in the Hamlin scoring books without ever having played for them.

"God, how embarrassing," Earl recalled as we warmed up before practice in the cafeteria. "I haven't been able to shake that humiliating stunt that afternoon even a year later."

That two point basket turned out to be one of a very few I was able to score my 8th grade year. Several of the players on our Hamlin team were taller than I was, and certainly, most were much better shooters. I began the season playing on second string as a forward behind Leo Bonilla, a wiry street fighter. He had been a starter as a 7th grader and was tough, several inches taller, and a reasonable shot. Despite that, I soon figured out how I could catch the coach's eye.

"Geez, I hate playing against you," Earl said one day at practice. "Everyone does. You're such a little pest." That comment only fueled my efforts. I realized then that probably my only chance of making the first string was to be a first class irritant, an aggressive, in-your-face type of player. I'd let the rest take care of itself.

By mid-season I had won a spot on the first string by making other players frustrated. I made it a point to slap dribbles into opposing players' shins, poke away passes, and gather impressive floor burns diving for every loose ball. None of these things involved my personal weakness, shooting. If I could just get the ball to my teammates who could shoot, I would be happy. Winning was what was most important to me.

Coach Carlile enjoyed that style of play. He had been a terrific basketball player at Marshfield High School in Coos Bay, a lightening quick guard who valued aggressive play. I was fortunate to have a coach like this early in my young basketball career.

One particularly tense game during that year pitted us against Cascade Jr. High of the Bethel district. Early in the season we had lost to Cascade at Hamlin quite decisively. It was our first loss. When we played them again at Cascade the following week, the tension was high on both sides. The game turned out to be a seesaw affair that came down to the final possession. With less than a minute to play Delmar Dykes, our rugged center tipped in a shot and we were up two points, 27-29. Cascade had the ball and with time ticking away arched a long outside shot which clanged off the back rim. Mickey "Stretch" Robinson, our string bean forward with gigantic hands, corralled the rebound but was called for a foul sending Cascade to the free throw line.

I glanced at the scoreboard. Only 28 seconds remained on the clock. The little Cascade guard we had nicknamed "Birdie" (because of his molded auburn DA) made the first free throw of a two-shot free throw opportunity.

Coach Carlile called time out. He gave us our final instructions on how he wanted us to handle the time remaining depending on whether they made or missed their last free throw.

The horn sounded ending the time out period and sent us back out onto the floor. Birdie's second shot hit the front rim, the back rim, and bounced to the top of the backboard before dropping down and through the basket tying the score.

Sensing the urgency but keeping his wits about him, Delmar quickly grabbed the ball and inbounded to Jerry Hollens who raced down court to the top of our key. Coach Carlile had called for a guard pick and roll, a quick play that involved our two best shooters, Jerry and Butch Cluff. They ran the play as instructed, but the ball got tipped toward the deep right baseline corner and into the hands of Earl who, not realizing that we still had time to reset the play, took two steps toward the basket and heaved up a 20 foot prayer. As soon as the shot left Earl's hands, Coach Carlile spun in a half circle away from the court and facing the bench, slammed his polished right wing-tip on the floor.

"Oh, no!" That angry scowl quickly switched to a Cheshire-like grin as the ball swished through the net. Coach Carlile frantically windmilled his arms yelling for us to get back on defense, but as Cascade inbounded the ball the buzzer sounded. Their last-second shot resulted in a desperation heave from 70 feet away. Nothing but air.

This game was the first time I had ever been involved in such a nail biter. All the way home on the bus I grinned as I replayed the pained expression on the coach's face when Earl's shot was launched. Then that pain flashing to a huge smile as the Earl's prayer was miraculously answered. And I heard again the classic coach line coming from Carlile's mouth: "Oh, no, no, no…Nice shotttt!"

Flirting with the "Hoers"

*"I picked beans, strawberries, filberts, blackcaps,
and also hoed weeds in the mint fields. My dad had so much
fun telling people his daughter was working as a "hoer"
for the summer to earn money for school clothes."*
Joy Reid, The Register-Guard, Sept. 18, 2011

Most of the kids I knew worked during the summer to earn money to buy their school clothes. The jobs readily available for us as adolescents were babysitting or picking cherries, strawberries, or beans. Girls did most of the babysitting which they claimed usually paid 35-50 cents an hour depending on the family and number of kids. The big employers, though, for most of us were the bean fields, and there were lots of bean fields, over 30 in the Eugene-Springfield area alone. The two I picked at were Wicklund's and Chase's. The first was near the end of Deadmond Ferry Road, and the other just over the railroad tracks ¼ mile north of home.

Most bean fields in the late '50s paid 2½ cents a pound for picked beans. Practicing our mental multiplication, we calculated that if we picked an average of 100 pounds a day and worked for seven weeks, pretty much the full season, we'd make close to $100. *(In today's world that would be upwards of about $750 in purchasing power.)* If we were good workers and stayed the full season, we got a couple of bonuses. The first was an additional ¼ cent per pound which was figured into our final check, and the other was the satisfaction of tearing down the bean vines on the last day. The latter, by itself, was worth staying the season.

On the very last bean-picking day in August of 1959, Dee and her sister Barb had the row right next to Bruce and me. We each picked our first sections clean then carried our metal five-gallon buckets to the next section. The four of us ran back to the first cedar post. Barb and Bruce lined up at the start of their respective rows. Eying his target, Bruce pawed the ground several times with his Converse All Stars like a cornered bull. He snuffled and shook his head.

"Three, two, one, go," Dee and I shouted. Arms held wide they tore into the section like Pamplona bulls, ripping vine after vine to the ground, pulling up just short of the second cedar post. Then they both stepped into the newly created opening and picked the leftover clinging vines from their hair and shirts.

"Ahh, that feels so good," laughed Barb. The satisfaction came from ridding ourselves of all the early morning starts, usually around 7:00 o'clock, when the scratchy vines were covered with dew. Even when we wore long-sleeved shirts to protect ourselves, the sleeves got soaked and felt like hundreds of wet, wriggling ant legs. It was all I could do not to yank my shirt off. If we came in just t-shirts, our arms would get an itchy rash from the raspy spines on the leaves and vines. We soon finished section two and Dee and I were given our turns.

"Red rover, red rover, send Mark and Dee right over," shouted Barb as she and Bruce stood at the beginning of the section three. I took off and, blinded by a pile of vines, was yanked away at the last moment from smashing into the cedar post.

"Whnppph. Easy big fella," Bruce said channeling his best Hollywood rendition of Silver's neigh and the Lone Ranger's response. He helped me pull the clinging leaves and vines off my face and shirt. I turned around to check on Dee. She had made it through the first third of the section but had gotten tangled in the vines.

"Darned vines," shouted Dee picking herself up off the ground. She stomped back a few steps and took another run at it. In all fairness, Dee was about five feet tall and couldn't have weighed more than 80 pounds. We were all taller and had another 40-50 pounds on her. If Bruce, Barb and I were like three Harley Davidsons attacking the vines, Dee was a Big Wheel tricycle. Nevertheless, legs churning and arms swinging, Dee made it to the end of the section.

For the next three hours we picked the beans and ripped down section after section. In one section we slipped in a muddy dip in the row and toppled to the ground. Another time I got delayed in an almost fitting conclusion to our wreckage. In a section near the end of the row, I hit a patch infested with slimy aphids. The impact of me hitting the vines left them slathered over my shirt and hands. I ran back to the mud and smashed the little bugs, scrubbing them quickly off my hands and shirt with the wet dirt.

When we finally did complete the row we were a sight to behold, but we were smiling. All that was left was to turn in our buckets and haul our burlap sacks to the scales for the final weigh in.

Plodding up the row I made sure to drag my sack through the mud a couple times to add a few more pounds. Then, after having everything weighed, we grabbed our lunches, rinsed our hands at the hand pump, and headed to the shade of the large fir trees on the north side of the bean yard.

The four of us plopped down in the trampled golden field grass below the outstretched arms of the trees. We dug into our

588-Pound Record For Beanpicking By Marilyn Burch

Marilyn Burch, 17, Rt. 4, Box 142, is champion bean-picker this week with the high of 588 pounds for one day.

Second high is Judy Mallam, 17, 137 West H st., with a total of 511.

With the weather cooling off, it is hoped someone can top last year's 600-pound record set by Rickey McDuffie at the Dewey Ray yard. Call results to the Springifeld News, RI 6-1671.

brown paper bags and unwrapped our sandwiches. It wasn't long before we were joined by Karla Dodd and Collette Peters, and right on their heels came Bill Reese and Tommy Johnson. The additions were interesting.

Karla, a short brunette was easy to get along with and could slug people with the best of them. Guys learned to stay clear of her swing. Collette, her picking partner, was a broad shouldered blonde who attracted stares like a candle flame attracts moths. Bill was talkative and quick witted, but long-legged thin like the two Ls in his name. Tommy joked and laughed easily. His dark eyes constantly danced with questions. It always seemed there was something he wasn't saying but wanted to ask.

"So how you going to spend all your money, Dee?" said Tommy.

"Oh, I figure I've now got enough to get a cherry Coke at Risher's, a couple 45s at Light's, and maybe a pair of flats at Leeds. That'll pretty much drain my cache."

"What about you, Tommy?" shot back Dee.

"I'm buying that red '57 Chevy hardtop on Cochran's lot. Nothing but the best for me."

"Good luck, Tommy. According to my calculations, at the rate you're filling those sacks you might be able to drive that home when you're about 28," said Bruce. The comments and wisecracks kept coming, a natural letdown for a summer's worth of work. Then the focus shifted.

"Hey, you guys, what do you say to washing this bean field season off? How about a quick splash in the river?" said Dee. With that we all got up and raced down to the nearby McKenzie. Leading the way, Dee waded in.

"Come on, you old poops," she teased. Not wanting to be shown up by a girl, I waded in next followed by Bruce and Collette. Tommy came last. The water, though mid August, was bone-numbing cold. Once we were all in above our ankles, Dee reached down and splashed water all down the front of Bruce. Bruce lunged and grabbed hold of Dee's arms.

"You're going down." With that he pulled Dee backward and slowly but surely lowered her into eight inches of McKenzie River water. She screamed and laughed and vowed to get even. That wasn't necessary as Bruce, stumbling to maintain his balance, stepped backward onto a mossy rock and fell onto his left side like a torpedoed ship. The dominoes had begun to fall. In a tussle Barb and I wound up on our knees trying to empty the river on each other. Tommy looked at Collette. Collette grinned then spun and made a futile race for shore, but Tommy pounced ensuring no one would escape the cleansing.

When, ten minutes later, we finally stepped up on the small sandy river's edge none of us had one dry hair or stitch of dry clothing. All of us were cleaner, refreshed, and smiling, our bodies clearly outlined by the clinging clothes. Left behind in the sparkling clear chilly water were the mud, sweat, and aphids. Also the memories of clanking of metal buckets, bean fights, and the sun-warmed burlap sacks.

Collecting our lunch sacks beneath the fir trees I caught a glimpse of Karla and Bill emerging from the tall grass field about 30 yards away. They had opted for a warmer, drier escapade. Both seemed to be smiling and a bit disheveled. Bruce caught my sight line and shook his head. Ah, *Peyton Place* had nothing on us.

Fashionistas and the Fashion Police

Wednesday, August 13, 1959. By my reckoning it was about 1:30 in the afternoon. After we had dried off a bit from our refreshing dip in the McKenzie, we grabbed what remained of our lunches and headed towards the bean field. Mrs. Wilkens, the bean boss, was waiting to greet us as we exited our trashed rows.

"Thanks for staying the whole season," she said. "You can pick up your checks at the house this coming Saturday morning after 9:00." We waved goodbye and trotted off to where our bikes were parked underneath a grove of trees on the south side of the bean yard. When we had all mounted our two-wheelers, Dee. Barb, Bruce, and I pedaled up Game Farm Road towards town. Five minutes later I peeled off at my house and waved goodbye to my three friends.

On the ride home we had agreed to meet at the pool for an evening swim to officially bring the curtain down on another bean season. It was our Labor Day celebration a bit early. The pool was the ideal summer hangout, a guaranteed mutual admiration society for those in the pool or on the surrounding bleachers. The guys could show off their cannonball techniques in the pool for the girls who laughed and applauded. The girls, much to the guys' delight, paraded along the pool deck or by the bleachers in their shorts or swimming suits. The celebration was over by 9:30 as our rides arrived, and we headed home.

Saturday morning, by arrangement, I waited for Bruce and mentally calculated the amount I thought I had earned toiling that summer in the bean yard. My goal was a mythical hundred dollars which would all go to buying the bulk of my school clothes for the coming year. Others who stayed 8-10 hours a day, not my usual 5-6, would make much more. I didn't care. I had baseball practice and needed my beauty rest. I was a growing boy.

A few minutes after 9:00 Bruce rolled down my driveway and knocked at the back door.

"Hey, Perdue, you going to bring your newspaper bag to carry all that cash home?" I waved him off and grabbed my bike.

"That rear rack of yours, Wofford, must be for the 8 bars of gold you're expecting, I suppose."

"Actually, I think most of my haul will fit right here," Bruce said tapping his rear Levi jeans pocket. He was fairly close to guessing the amount of loot we would each get, a few numbers written on a small paper check.

We nosed our bikes out onto the county road and leisurely made our way to the old Chase farmhouse. When we clunked back down the steps about 10 minutes later we each held a sealed white envelope. We reached our bikes and quickly tore the envelopes open.

"About what I figured," I said. "Just a few measly pounds short of my $100. How'd you do?"

"I got $86. 22," Bruce answered. "But I made about $9 holding ladders for MaryAlice and Arlene during cherry picking. Now I just have to make some decisions about what to buy. I'm going down to Alexander's later today and see what they've got and how far this money will take me."

"I've got baseball games this afternoon and tomorrow so I don't think I'll be able to look till next week. If I don't find what I like at Alexander's I'm going to poke around in Eugene and maybe hold some aside for The Gay Blade. Why don't you call me tonight and let me know what you found. I know I have to get some shoes at Alexander's or across the street at McElhany's."

"OK, talk to you tonight," Bruce said. True to his word the phone rang a little after 7:00.

"It's for you, Mark," Mom said. "Don't be long. I'm expecting a call in a few minutes." I grabbed the phone and stretched the long cord into the bathroom for a bit of privacy.

"So, what'd you find?" I asked. "Any good deals?

"Alexander's has some great sales going on. You can get two pair of polished cotton pants for $5.00. They had black, brown, and a light cream color," said Bruce. I got a couple of short-sleeve plaid shirts to match the pants. They were half off. If you want long sleeve there's a bunch of them for 99 cents each. Socks were three pairs for a dollar. What kind of shoes were you thinking of?"

"I think a pair of black loafers. I still have a pretty good pair of suede desert boots from last year. I might get a pair of low-cut black Chuck Taylor tennies. I'll just have to see how my money holds out. Shoes will take a big bite out of my check. I hate having to spend so much of my money on shoes," I said. There was a polite tap-tap-tap on the bathroom door.

"OK, Mark, time to get off. You've been on long enough. If you still have more to say you can call back later," Mom said.

I didn't call Bruce back. It was my turn to wash the evening dishes and after that I plopped down at the desk in my bedroom and began my shopping list, mentally allocating and spending my bean check money. On Monday I figured I would look at Alexander's and then go to downtown Eugene to check out the clothes at Penney's, Sears, and the more ritzy Gay Blade. By week's end I would have all the things I needed. I hoped to have some money left.

Three days before school started I realized I had a glaring fashion problem. All my new pants needed to be "pegged." The pants from the stores came with a straight untapered leg, and unless you wished to be a social outcast you needed to peg your pants. The fashion police had laws about this. I turned to my nearest seamstress.

"Mom, will you please fix these pants?" I pleaded. She looked at me with that exhausted one-more-thing smile.

"Sure. Go get the sewing machine and set it on the dining room table. I'll be right there." I ran to her bedroom closet and lifted the little portable Singer sewing machine case off the floor. I brought it to the table and took the black featherweight out of its case and plugged it in. Cruising into my bedroom I brought out my cream-colored poplin pants. In a few minutes Mom appeared.

"So, what are we doing with these pants, Mark?"

"I need to have them pegged," I said. "See how wide these things are. I can almost stick both my legs down one of these pant legs. They're way too floppy."

"Well, how much do you want me to taper them?" she asked.

"Everybody's wearing them about six inches wide at the bottom," I said. Mom gave me that you've-got-to-be kidding-me half smile.

"Let's make it eight inches," she said. I was about to protest but then thought better of it. Since she was going to do it, I just let it go. At least I could probably blend in with the cool kids and not stand out as having just dropped in from 1942.

"OK, fine with me," I said and watched as she turned the pants legs inside out and chalked lines from the pockets to the cuff, measuring and pinning the fabric. Then she ran the sewing machine down the lines, reinforced the cuff, and pulled the pants back to the way they should be.

"Now go put these on and come back so I can take a look at you before we cut off any of the excess material," she said. I hurried into the back bedroom and changed into my new pants. They were still a little wide for my taste but a definite improvement. When I showed up with a smile Mom made me turn around a couple times, tugged at my cuffs, and gave me her seal of approval.

"Alright," she said. "From now on you're on your own. If you want any more of your pants tapered, you know how to do it. I'll be happy to answer your questions, but you're doing the sewing."

The next afternoon I did just that. I pegged both my black and dark brown polished cotton pants to six-inch leg openings.

Then I put the black ones on with my new short-sleeve white, black, and blue plaid shirt and cruised around the house. When Dad caught a glimpse of my sewing he just shook his head.

"That the new style, Mark?" he asked. "You look like a zoot suiter in those pants." I didn't know what that was, but by his lopsided grin I somehow felt like he was ribbing me about my taste in clothing. I didn't care. He wasn't the one trying to blend in with all the kids at school.

Almost every guy, even the Neanderthal Lenny Poole, still had his pants pegged. Sometimes though, if you weren't careful those pants could be your worst enemy. Earl told me that one day Jerry Hollens lost track of time because he was out holding hands with Suzanne Jeffries in the breezeway. With one minute to go he raced into the locker room to get dressed down for PE. In the rush he panicked and got both his feet stuck in the narrow openings of his pants. By the time he struggled out to the PE line where JC was taking roll it was too late. Showing up tardy earned you a hack, and Jerry got his buns well toasted.

A couple nights later when I had gotten my pants fixed to my liking I had a dream. A fire had erupted in the boy's gym. At the time I was in the PE showers. When the fire alarm siren began its whine I raced dripping wet from the shower and yanked open my gym locker. I jammed my wet feet into the narrow pants legs. Cussing and yelling at my plight, I began inhaling smoke and started to lose consciousness. I snapped awake in a deep sweat from my dream. Because of those pegged pants I had nearly died in that fire.

The other fashion requirements for a guy were a narrow half-inch wide black suede belt, the buckle worn rotated to the side, and white socks. Nothing but white socks. Looking at the newspaper ads for guys and pictures in my brother's yearbook I saw black loafers, brown and white saddle shoes, or maybe a few hold over English brogues, but the gap between the tops of those shoes and the bottom of the pants would be stark white. If you wanted to be in the in crowd, that is.

When I had finished all my shopping Bruce and I went searching for one last thing, a coat. Nothing hanging in the stores caught our attention, at least nothing we could afford. I searched the newspapers and watched the TV ads. I just knew I needed something durable, warm, and something I wouldn't feel out of place wearing. The Thursday afternoon ads that week in *The Springfield News* provided a possible way out of this dilemma. I called Bruce that night.

"Hey, big guy. Have you looked at the Springfield paper today?"

"Nah, Mark, I just got home. What'd you find?"

"Well, go get the paper. Look at the bottom right corner of page four." I waited. Bruce, huffing a bit, picked the phone back up.

"OK, got it." I heard the rustling of paper.

"You talking about Archie's store?" he said.

"Yeah, check out the jackets." The line went quiet except for Bruce's breathing.

"Wow," those might be so cool!" Bruce sounded excited. "And only ten bucks. Let's go check them out this weekend, OK?"

What Bruce and I had seen were navy blue "bomber jackets" at the Eugene Surplus Store. Later that Saturday Bruce and I forked over the money and walked away with our wardrobe completed. The best part was that I still had nearly $17 dollars left from my summer money. That and I had a "neat" jacket.

A couple times when I was browsing for clothes I saw Dee and some of her friends also shopping at Alexander's. They picked up a few things and then expanded their search. Some of them hopped the dark green city bus to check out the Eugene stores because of the bargains they could get. And sometimes their parents had no idea that their daughters were such bargain hunters. I found this out the first week of school when all the girls were showing off their purchases.

"My mom was concerned that I get good shoes so that I wouldn't ruin my feet, so she gave me $10 and orders to go to Burch's in Eugene," said Emily. "Suzanne and I hopped a city bus – "

"You mean you didn't ride your bikes or have your parents take you?" I asked.

"Just let me finish, would you?" barked Emily. "We had too many packages to carry and I didn't want my mom to know how I was spending her money. Besides, have you ever tried to ride a bike in a skirt? We went to Leeds instead and got several pairs of flats for the money, each costing us only $2.99. Annie bought a nice Ship and Shore blouse down the street at The Broadway. I think it was also $2.99. We went to Eugene because the Springfield stores didn't have as big a selection."

I knew Donna, a neighborhood friend, used to love going with her mom to The Bon Marche for the end-of-the-month sales. She only got paid 85 cents an hour working at the Arctic Circle so she really looked for good buys.

The other Eugene draws for us kids were the JC Penney department store and the Sears department store. Because our summer money was so hard to part with, we did a lot of comparison shopping.

For the girls, the one solution for saving money while adding to their wardrobe was to sew their own. Guys didn't do that, but most junior highs at that time offered Home Ec. classes that taught girls to cook and sew. Many girls took advantage of that. One day I overheard Annie and Emily in Ms. Enns' English class talking about what they had actually learned. Annie Settlemeyer, it turns out, was really appreciative of Mrs. Cornelius.

"She taught me how to make white sauce. Now every time Mom asks me to help with dinner I think of Mrs. Cornelius, especially if the meal includes a sauce. I learned how to measure ingredients for baking and cooking and how to properly handle food.

"You must be getting to be quite the little chef," I said.

"Well, I was hoping to avoid killing anyone in my family," she laughed. Cornelius's sewing projects also resulted in Annie and her Mom taking off on shopping trips together.

"Mom helped me in buying the perfect material for the best price. I always felt that it was important that I look just like everyone else, but a little different. Choosing the fabrics and sewing your own clothes makes that possible."

When I bragged that by my scrupulous shopping I still had $17 left from my summer work, Emily couldn't help sharing her cost-cutting secrets.

"Well, smarty pants, Annie's right. If we decide to sew our own clothes we can really save money, almost half of what we'd have to pay in the store. For instance, the wool plaid skirt I see in the store windows for $8.98 I can make for $4.98. This includes the zipper, thread, and pattern. Plus, I get to choose the material and pattern I like. Heath's has all its fabric on sale right now. Since I babysat this summer I didn't make quite as much as you guys, so I'm counting my pennies."

The girls were pretty smart, I had to admit, and they definitely knew what fashions were the ones they wanted to be wearing. For girls at this time, knee-length full skirts and matching cardigans with white blouses was a standard outfit. Whether the skirts were cotton prints or box pleated wool, it was skirts and dresses that hung in their closets. No jeans, slacks, or shorts were permitted as school wear. To go with those full skirts another essential was the brightly colored crinolines that made the skirt flare out, emphasizing a narrow waist. Not that any of us guys needed additional assistance. We were already acutely aware of female contours.

I never much thought anything about crinolines till the day I witnessed a "cat fight" in a Hamlin breezeway. I was just an 8th grader on my way to my wood shop class trying hard to steer clear of the behemoth 9th graders hogging the passageways. About 20 feet in front of me, smack dab in the middle of the breezeway, a buxom 9th grade girl was talking to an intent 9th grade boy. Her arm was hooked through his. She was wearing a white blouse, print full cotton skirt, and matching red cardigan sweater. As I neared where she was standing batting her eyelashes, a blue female blur shot by me and screeched to a stop right in front of the amorous pair.

"You bitch," she screamed. Everyone in the breezeway froze, heads rotating to the site of the confrontation. In the next five seconds I saw red, lots of it. The blonde-haired blue blur of a screamer lifted her target's full cotton skirt, grabbed handfuls of red crinoline and yanked them to grey cement breezeway surface, then stomped off. Aghast, the girl in the red cardigan hiked up her crinolines and rushed off to the nearest restroom to repair the damage. I didn't know either girl. I made a note to steer clear of the blue screamer if ever I were to encounter her in the future. She was a wild one. I could only guess that this was one those hormone-induced rages that proved "two is a couple, three is a crowd."

Hick's Party

Date,Feb.24,1961

Time,7:30-11:30

Place,1267 Darlene Ave.

Refreshments,pop,potatoe chips,

PEOPLE

1. Kneeland-Bates
2. Garrett-Haugen
3. McGuire-Ebbert
4. Bryson-Shupe
5. Hicks-Chruszch
6. Laxton-Moore
7. McMahon-Tofflemoyer
8. Webb-Byrnes
9. Mock-BARNS
10. Tennett- Christianson
11. Burrell-
12. Davis-

Parties: Into the Social Wading Pool

The first month of junior high I had to shift gears. I had been, much to my delight, thrown into a new world of hands-on learning. For me this meant designing and then making a leather wallet in Arts and Crafts and a lathe-turned wooden bowl in shop. In nearby classrooms band students pushed valves, pressed keys, and struck drums. Girls sewed dresses and cooked meals in Home Ec. We exercised and showered every day in PE and then burned off our lunches with noontime dances. During the rest of the day it was school as usual with science, math, social studies, and English. It was a full day of listening, learning, and doing.

The hands-on learning, however, didn't end when the clock struck 3:00 and school was out for the day. There was more. This realization came as MaryAlice Monihan, the smiling poster child for male adolescent fantasies, brushed into me as I exited Miss Sloan's first period class. I was admiring the shiny red plastic heart in my right palm and not really paying attention to the frenetic breezeway traffic. I had just pulled the glossy pendant from the burnishing wheel.

"Oh, sorry," I said. She laughed and extended a small white envelope to me. I took it, stared at her for a few seconds, then tucked it quickly in my notebook.

"See you," she said over her shoulder then scooted down the breezeway in the opposite direction. When I got into Mr. Barrow's science class I squeezed into my desk and withdrew the envelope from the pencil pouch in my binder. "Mark" was written in round bubbly letters on the front of the envelope in turquoise ink. I pried back the glued flap and pulled out a small card. *You're Invited,* it said. Opening the card a sudden electricity rippled through my body. It was as if the sun had splashed across my shoulders on a chilly morning.

According to the card I had been invited to a party thrown by Emily Vinson the coming Friday night from 7-10. The invitations said to wear school clothes. Refreshments would be provided. I didn't know what to think. I had only been to one school party in my life. That was an all-school skating party at the roller rink in Glenwood in 6th grade. I definitely needed to talk to Dee Howell, my bean picking buddy who had helped me numerous times my first couple weeks. She always seemed to have her social stethoscope plugged in to the pulse of things at school. Or maybe Bruce Wofford or Earl Dwyer would be able to clue me in. Surely they were veterans when it came to things like this.

Then I got to thinking. What if one or both of those guys hadn't been invited. I imagined walking up to Dwyer and saying, "Hey, did you get invited to the party?" And him saying, "What party?" Yeah, that probably wouldn't be the brightest move on my part. No, I decided, I'd better find MaryAlice. She was the one who started all this. So at lunch, when the noon dance music began and I could pry her away from her admirers, I asked her to dance.

"What's the invitation about? I mean I get it, but what am I supposed to do? I feel kind of awkward. I really don't know that many kids yet."

"Oh, Mark. Just relax. You know plenty of the kids who will be there. You play football with some of the guys, and you've got many of the girls in your classes," she said. "We thought it would be good to get to know you a bit better. Besides, you're a good dancer and there will be a lot of that. You'll have a great time. And I get at least one dance – if the other girls will let me have one." She winked.

On the way to 5th period after the lunchtime dance I replayed our exchange. *We thought it would be good to get to know you better. Who was the "we"?*

The week whizzed by me on roller skates and before I knew it Friday had arrived. Through notes, phone calls, and conversations I learned that both Bruce and Earl had been invited. That eased my anxiety a bit. They appeared almost as nervous about the party as I was. I also learned that in planning the party Emily and MaryAlice decided which girls they'd like to be at the party. Those girls were then paired with a boy that the girl wanted to invite. Some of the people at the party were already an item; others were unattached but hopeful. Bruce and I were in the latter group. Earl was in the former.

Dad dropped me at Emily's, and her parents met me at the door. They took my coat and led me into the living room. Emily, Dee, and MaryAlice came to greet me. Music was playing and kids were bundled in small groups talking. I found Bruce and walked over next to him. After a bit of kidding and joking we found our way to the chips and pop and settled into the flow of the conversations and music. I danced several fast dances with various girls I felt comfortable asking, and a couple slow dances as well. Mostly what I was doing was observing and taking mental notes, learning how this game was played.

One of the things I found interesting was that the size of the individuals paired up to dance seemed to make absolutely no difference. I watched Willie McAllister slow dancing with MaryAlice. The top of his blond head barely reached her shoulders. When Willie and MaryAlice danced she could count the hairs on the crown of his head. He could stare at the third button from the top of her white cotton blouse. She didn't seem to mind; I'm sure he didn't either. I secretly wished I was Willie.

On the other hand, Earl was almost the same height as the gorgeous strawberry blonde he seemed to be targeting. When they laughed at each other's jokes their eyes met. When they danced slowly cheek to cheek to Frankie Avalon's *Venus* a mutual attraction seemed to be taking place. I didn't know this sudden interest of Earl's, but I was enjoying the view. She was a sculpted beauty. After the dance Earl sat down by me and I had to ask. My curiosity was killing me.

"Who's the girl you were dancing with?" I asked?

"Ah, that's Julia Weston. She moved here last year from North Carolina. I think she's so pretty...and so far ahead of me. I'm just a hick from Springfield barely knowing how to complete a circle on the dance floor, and it's like she's already been to Miss USA Finishing School. God, I feel so stupid sometimes. But I can dream, can't I?"

She did seem elegant and a bit more sophisticated, sort of like a cross between Rita Haworth and what I had seen painted on the nose of a WW II bomber. While I was considering what it would have been like to be Earl, Emily brought out a broom handle.

"OK everybody, it's time to try your limbo skills. How low can you go?" With that she put on a Chubby Checker limbo record and we all lined up. I made it through the first and second times, but on the third time I knocked the bar off. As I picked myself off the floor and walked over to stand next to Bruce on the side of the room, Earl sauntered over.

"Mark, your barn door's open," he mumbled under his breath. Holy cow. *I haven't been this embarrassed since the same thing happened when I served as an altar boy for my cousins' wedding in second grade!* Nonchalantly I spun toward the wall and fixed the problem then turned on Earl.

"OK, how long have I been like this?" I asked.

"Hey, I wouldn't have even noticed since I was behind you in line, but I saw some of the girls looking at you. I wondered what the deal was so I gave you a once over. Once I discovered the problem I thought you'd be glad to know."

The rest of the crowd took turns falling on their backs as they attempted to negotiate the lowering bar. In the end it was little Willie McAllister sneaking under the bar last and being declared the winner. That's how the party ended. I left gladly, anxious to bury my head under a pillow, dreading school on Monday.

Bruce Wofford, the music wizard, also had a couple of small parties at his house. Typical of adolescence, Bruce wanted to be like everyone else but, of course, just a little bit different. So, instead of holding his party in the living room of the modest two-story house his dad had built on Waverly Street, he held it upstairs in his party room.

The party room, a former pool room, was almost a mirror image of his 9 x 12 bedroom with a few notable exceptions, the first being it's unique coloration. The day I first walked into the room I felt like I had just fallen into a first grader's Crayola box. It had one flat-black graffiti wall; the others were red, blue, and green. The floor was painted yellow. A multi-colored Don Martin-like character from *Mad* magazine graced the pink party door.

"My cousin is a talented artist," Bruce explained. "He agreed to help with the cartoon." Arced across the door above the character were the words "I Like It Like That." The wording had come from a song by the same name. A line from that song was "... *and the name of the place was, I like It like that.*"

A box full of colored chalk sat on one of the nightstands by the black wall. First time visitors were encouraged to "sign in, please," just like the *What's My Line* television show or leave a bit of graffiti on the wall. After a couple of years of visitors the wall was a crammed with running conversations and comments. It was a real attraction, even if it did smack of Dobie Gillis and Maynard G. Krebs, a couple of Bruce's favorites.

"When my parents asked why in the heck I painted the room like this I told them, 'I like it like that.' That's my story and I'm sticking to it," he said.

The wall and upstairs setting made this party room different. What also made Bruce's place memorable was one particular April evening there. The party had been rolling along for a couple of hours and the initial buzz had worn off. Lights had dimmed, the music had grown softer, and a few of the couples had wound themselves into knots. I had gone downstairs to find the bathroom and had just begun my climb back up the stairs – most of my friends' houses had only one bathroom – when I heard a loud shriek.

"Hey, what kind of a girl do you think I am?" Just then Lonnie Majors, a trim, well-endowed brunette, bounded past me down the stairs. I continued upward. As I cleared the last step the room flickered back to normal illumination and several entwined couples sprang upright, adjusting their clothes and fluffing their hair. Bruce slipped *Love Potion #9* on the turntable. The mood changed.

I never found out exactly what happened with Lonnie that night, but the following Monday Bruce slipped me a note that got right to the point. "You should see what Lonnie had to say about Earl. It's on my board in red and it's still smoking. Might want to bring a fire extinguisher when you drop by next time." That only piqued my curiosity so at lunch I found Earl.

"Hey, what happened with Lonnie?" I asked. "Bruce said she was pretty hot about it."

"Nothing, really," Earl said. "Maybe I got a bit too frisky. What's a guy to do? I just couldn't help myself. Anyway, at least my mom wasn't there." Earl proceeded to remind me of the night I had hosted a party and Mom, cruising through the living room and not finding me attending to my host duties, became suspicious. She began scouring the house. Unfortunately she found Emily, Earl, A.J. and me in the back bedroom otherwise engaged.

"I remember her words so clearly," Earl said. "'A little more dancing. A little more dancing, please.' How embarrassing. So don't get on me about Lonnie. She's gorgeous, funny, and certainly worth the effort. I'm not giving up on that just yet." *Yeah, that's probably the truth. That would be so unlike you, and one of the reasons life around you is never dull.*

And then there was the party queen, MaryAlice. Her house was probably the most famous because she threw more parties than anybody else. She had the perfect set up: a spacious room set off the main house behind their carport. Linoleum tile covered the floor making it easy to dance on and easy to clean. This party room had its own bathroom. We could turn up the music and be rowdy. Because of the room's separation from the house the noise wouldn't bother her parents. In fact, her parents checked in now and then, but felt comfortable leaving us pretty much to ourselves.

The room also contained a couch, a console piano and several large comfy chairs scattered about. Music was provided by a portable record player covered in a turquoise and white leatherette. It had a plastic column about the diameter of a 50-cent piece that fitted down over the spindle to enable the listener to play 45s. Partygoers often brought their favorite records.

Usually there were no more than 12-14 kids at a party, always even numbers as kids were invited as existing couples or as rumored possibilities. This was the party host or hostess's attempt at matchmaking. These parties always started the same as the ballroom dancing units in junior high PE classes. Boys clustered together on one side of the room, girls on the other. It was a safety-of-the-herd, circle-the-wagons mentality.

But once the skids were greased – usually by the girls dancing together as partners or coming across in small groups to grab guys and drag them out on he floor – everything was fine. If MaryAlice's parents dropped in to replenish snacks and talk with the kids things reverted to the appropriate volume and behavior. Once the parents exited, though, the volume and craziness resumed.

Every once in a while other interruptions occurred. Usually, it was some female crisis – a bra strap or slip showing – that sent a cluster of girls to the small bathroom to work through the drama.

One Saturday night Jimmy, an oversized garden gnome and class charmer, showed up giving his best academy performance of being drunk. Immediately two or three girls flitted sympathetically around him listening to his tale of woe, soothingly reassuring him that things would be all right and letting him know that they felt his pain. Butch Cluff, taking in the performance, mumbled that Jimmy had gotten most of what he had come for, attention. Jimmy obviously wasn't getting it from Mary Alice, the heartthrob of his life. At the time she was busy looking dreamily into Derek's Macklin's eyes, her arms wrapped around his neck as Timi Yuro cried, *"I'm so hurt/ To think you lied, you lied to me."*

Do you think he's drunk?" Arlene Kingsbury, MaryAlice's best friend, leaned over to ask Bruce and me.

"No way," said Bruce quoting his favorite band teacher. "He's about as drunk as one could be from being hit on the backside with a wet bar towel." But this daring venture to the dark side of social acceptability (smoking cigarettes or drinking beer) represented how desperate Jimmy was.

In the same boat but more hopeful than Jimmy were those of us who were not already linked to someone. We had been invited as friends of the hostess with the possibility that somehow a magical connection or two might be made before the evening was over. Seated on a chair next to the console piano I considered the possibilities. Then, unable to decide on my next move, I opted for some potato chips and half ham sandwich. Much safer.

When I returned to my seat by the piano, Annie Settlemeyer, a curvy strawberry blonde, and Dee Howell, the perky brunette energy bundle, were sitting on the previously unoccupied piano bench a couple feet to my right. We traded a few awkward questions then, having exhausted our supply, settled into an uncomfortable silence. I had begun to tense up when from across the room laughter and loud greetings erupted. Bruce had arrived. He glanced around the room, waved at me and, grabbing a small folding chair, headed my way. I exhaled the breath I didn't realize I had been holding. My pulse slowed. As he plopped down in front of the piano Dee and Annie barraged him with questions.

"Geez, Brucie, what took you so long?" said Dee.

"Yeah, the party started 15 minutes ago!" added Annie.

"Well," Bruce responded, "I guess the big old fins on our '60 Buick need to be waxed again. They had a bit of trouble slicing through the humid air tonight. Either that or Dad was worried about getting a ticket for exceeding his 12 mph speed limit." Bruce always seemed to be blessed with all the right words. While all of this was going on MaryAlice, our hostess, had slipped over to the record player and stuck on a Bruce Wofford favorite sure to liven things up.

"Don't you know that I danced,
I danced till a quarter to three..."

That's all it took to end our conversation. Before I knew what was happening, Bruce jumped up as if Mary Alice had shot 240 volts through his metal folding chair, grabbed Annie, and bounded out into the center of the room. Dee grabbed my hand and yanked me up.

"Come on you old poop," she said leading me into the fray. She had used that expression numerous times in the bean yard. Slowly my reluctance began to dissolve. In less than three minutes the music ended and we headed back towards the piano. A driving guitar rift rattled the room followed by

"Wake up, little Susie, wake up,
Wake up little Susie, wake up..."

Wofford spun around and grabbed Dee's hand.

"Come on, you old poop," he said grinning. I looked at Annie and shrugged my shoulders.

"Wanna dance?" I didn't have a ready list of poop lines

"Sure," Annie said. This isn't so bad, I thought. Maybe I could do this. Once 10 or 12 kids got out on the floor spinning by one another the smart aleck comments began to emerge.

"Woohoo! Shake it, Arlene."

"Yeah, well, you just wish you had this swing in your back yard," Arlene mocked, playing the game.

"Actually I'd like to see the whole playground," shouted Bruce.

"Oh, you're so bad," said Connie, Arlene's Wayside Lane neighbor.

"Come on a my house, my house a come on," Arlene smirked keeping the tease going.

With the laughter a lot of the perceived barriers dropped and kids eagerly traded partners on the dance floor as fast dance song after fast dance song played. Then there was a break. A little sweaty and a bit drained we grabbed iced Pepsis from the cooler chest and gladly popped down.

"Speaking of bad," Bruce said remembering Connie's comment, "the only really bad girls here would be the ones bold enough to be wearing black underwear. My cousin told me that's the way you could tell the loose girls at the drive-ins."

"Haven't noticed that," I said, "but do you think Jimmy will actually drop those aspirins in MaryAlice's Coke like he said he was going to? You know he wouldn't be above doing about anything to swing her focus from Derrick." I just shook my head. What snapped me back to the moment was Elvis.

"Are you lonesome tonight
Do you miss me tonight?

Mary Alice, or one of her girlfriends, must have decided it was time to get serious. This was one of her all-time favorite songs. Seemed like she always loved those sad ones. It could just as easily have been Brenda Lee's *I'm Sorry* or Roy Orbison's *Crying*. Sure enough, out in the middle of the floor dancing couples began wrapping around each other like morning glories climbing fence posts. I sat clinging to my chair and Pepsi.

Ah, heck, I thought. No guts no glory. I turned to Annie, and pulled her up. With Dee already occupied, Bruce grabbed Norma Godwin, a new girl in our group. Not being recognized items like the other couples, there was ample daylight between our four insecure torsos as we faced our partners and began to dance. Hasty questions and answers were accompanied by polite laughter. As the 45 played on I considered the next step. Not being a veteran of the party scene, I began hoping for the best but anticipating the worst.

My internal arguments began. Should I make the move, pull her closer? No, she'll consider me a jerk and I'll later be a part of a girls' phone conversation. *"Oh, no, I don't like him. Well, maybe, but just as a friend."* Or maybe even the most crushing revelation, *"You know, he's like a brother to me."*

I didn't ask her to dance to be her brother. I could just hear Earl the Deviant pulling me aside. *"Look, chicken liver, you'll never know if you don't try."* Gritting my teeth I attempted to extinguish the daylight between our young bodies. Now, the next question, do I try for cheek to cheek?

The Deviant magically reappeared screaming in my ear, *"You've got the green light now, baby. Pedal to the metal."* Not wanting to risk losing my hard-earned success a voice in my head kept repeating, *"Don't press your luck, you dimwit. Just enjoy it and don't ruin this moment by stepping on her feet."* The faint but unmistakable fragrance of something like roses, carnations, and lilacs drifted across my face from her shiny shoulder-length hair. She smelled good.

All too soon Elvis ended his sad questions and we broke apart. I thanked her for the dance and she smiled.

"Sure," she replied. I fixated on the white box-pleated skirt that hugged her hips, the hem swaying back and forth as she turned and hurried to join the group at the record player. Snapping back to earth I returned to my partially consumed Pepsi. I couldn't wait to phone Bruce after the party. We could compare stories. The guys' versions.

I was quite sure when we got back to school Monday morning the grapevine would be humming. I imagined party-goers frenetically exchanging those little triangular notes like secret agent couriers ricocheting in a pin ball machine. I didn't know if I was a player in this game, but I had definitely begun enjoying the action.

Robin Hood and Skiptooth

The magic carpet ride to adventure and opportunity for older teenagers was the car. For junior high-age kids that carpet took the form of a time honored two-wheeler, the bicycle. City bus routes for Eugene and Springfield were minimal compared to larger cities. If you wanted to flee parental scrutiny and be on your own, kids hopped on their trusty balloon-tired, single-speed two-wheeler and sailed off to meet with friends, headed to the swimming pool, or grabbed a Coke at the local hangout.

We not only rode our bikes to school or social gatherings, but also to babysitting or the bean fields in the summer. When my older brother entered Hamlin in 9th grade and started organized sports, he didn't have time to do his paper route. He had delivered *The Springfield News* for three years during his 6th-8th grade at St. Al's. I inherited his paper route and for $25 I also got his bike, a spiffy 26 inch forest-green Raleigh Robin Hood. We usually referred to these skinny-tired imports like the Raleigh as English Racers. They got their "racer" name because they came equipped with snazzy 3-speed Sturmey Archer gearing and front handlebar mounted hand brakes.

Unlike the American bikes, these foreign bikes required regular maintenance. You had to periodically adjust the hand brake tension and replace the brake pads. You needed to lift a small cap on the rear axle and shoot a little oil in to keep the gears lubricated. You even sometimes needed to increase or decrease the tension on the shifter cable. If you didn't pay attention to that, you might slip into neutral instead of second gear. It was literally a male adolescent's first real acquaintance with hell should this surprise occur as he was upright and pumping hard while balanced over the top tube. These imports even came equipped with a generator that provided electricity for a headlight and taillight. In car terms, riding this bike was like driving a Jaguar while your friends were pedaling their Chevys and Fords. Mimicking expensive imported cars, many even came with a real leather seat.

The true workhorse of my bicycling days in junior high, however, was my 26" red-metallic J.C. Higgins Skiptooth, a lighter weight sporty American bike. It wasn't one of those fancy Cadillac-type bikes with fat balloon tires known as cruisers. They weighed a ton and had lights and battery powered push-button horns, shock absorbing front handlebar springs, and cargo racks over the rear fenders. My Skiptooth, as the name hints, was more like a stripped down 57 Chevy Bel Air. It came equipped with chrome wheels and handlebars, but was just a single speed with a Bendix coaster brake. I didn't have to adjust anything or spend hours fine tuning. I just got on and rode. I loved, after cleaning it up, seeing the sun strike the chrome wheels spraying flashing patterns onto the blacktop as I whizzed down the street.

I also thrilled in flying down a dirt road then standing up, leaning the bike over slightly, and slamming down on the pedal-brake while turning the handlebars. If I did this just right I could cut a wide arc in the dirt and send a big cloud of dust high in the air, just like professional racers do in all those car commercials on TV.

Bruce, the talented musician and wild-man dancer, took pride in his bike, too. It was a 24" maroon and white Schwinn. Unlike my minimalist red bike, his was a bit classier. Being on the top of the high tech curve at the time it had three speeds. Mastering this upscale technology, however, caused Bruce some problems at first. I called him when I learned he had gotten his Chrysler Imperial-type bike.

"Hey, Bruce. How you liking your new luxury bike?" I asked needling him a bit.

"Figuring out how to use the shifter and what the gears were for has taken me a while, but after a few weeks it'll probably become second nature to fly up and down the hills or go to high gear on long fast straight runs." Every week or so Bruce washed his bike, dried it off, and polished it to a sparkle.

"It's so neat having a cool bike," Bruce told me. "Right down to using an SOS pad to scrub the whitewall tires to make them whiter than other bikes. I did take the basket off my bike after discovering from an older boy, my friend's neighbor, that baskets were for sissies. There's a small rack over the back fender; that stayed after having passed the 'cool' test."

Since not everyone had a bike with them all the time, it was not unusual to give a friend a ride to wherever you were headed. There were several ways that kids could double up on a bike. The most common was for the passenger to sit side-saddle on the top tube, their rear end butted up against the handlebars. This way balance was easiest for the driver to handle, conversational distance was ideal, and the driver had reasonable control with both hands on the handle bars.

A second way was for the passenger to sit on the front handlebars facing forward. Steering wasn't as easy, and it was brutal for the passenger if the person doing the pedaling hit a pothole or big bump, but for short distances it could be as exciting as the best carnival ride. The thrill of the ride for the passenger depended on the how much of a wise guy the driver felt like being. Sometimes in the excitement accidents happened. And it wasn't only guys that were involved. In Mr. Renwick's class the spring of my 8th grade year, Annette Jensen showed me her scars. She seemed both embarrassed and proud.

"Before I entered Hamlin the older boys in our neighborhood were expert riders," said Annette. "It was a thrill to ride double with them. It always felt to me like they were out of control, but, of course, they weren't. Being out in the country we had gravel roads rather than blacktop, so the riding wasn't very smooth. I always marveled how they could slam those bikes around and make them do anything they wanted. It was when I got my horse that they didn't have a chance. I could outrun them all!

"I still have this scar on my Achilles where I got tangled up in the spokes. That possibility always scared me. More than once I fell off and bloodied my hands from landing on the gravel."

Sometimes necessity dictated a third option for doubling up. Earl Dwyer and I worked on perfecting this method one day.

"I don't know what prompted this ordeal," he said, "but it was probably just another one of those moronic things I did." Earl was visiting me at my house on Game Farm Rd. and we were trying to figure out a way to get out to Goshen to see Annette. A timely connection in Earl's grey matter reminded him that he had the keys to his grandfather's Jeep which was sitting at his house up in the Mohawk Valley. Looking around, the only transportation at our disposal at that moment was a two-wheeled pain mobile belonging to Karla Dodd. Earl had relieved two guys of her bike – they had "borrowed it" from her in the bean yard – and he had ridden it to my house.

"Now the logical thing for me to do was to go get the jeep, but knowing how misery loves company, you volunteered to go along double. We were creative. We took turns pedaling. One of us pedaled while the other one rode, first on the handle bars then on the seat." It wasn't long before Earl's grey matter sparked another connection.

"Funny, but I remembered it being a lot shorter in a car," Earl said when we were about halfway to his house. Somewhere past the point of no return we discovered why.

"I wondered why all this seemed so difficult," Earl said looking where the rubber met the road. Naturally we had never bothered to even look at the air in those weather-cracked tires. We were just short of riding on the rims.

"Think I might have been in a hurry?" He shook his head. We finally made it to Earl's "manor on the Mohawk" as he jokingly called it, jumped in the Jeep, and shot off to Goshen. After visiting Annette for all of 15 minutes we headed the Jeep back to Earl's house. A few miles from the garage I got a sinking feeling. We still needed to pedal back to town.

"I think I would have been smarter just to run those 18 miles," said Earl. We did remember to air up the tires for the ride back, thank God, but we must have looked really silly. "And did I mention that the pile of rust was a GIRLS bike." *Man, the things a guy like Earl would do for love.*

And just to show that those adolescent hormones were a shared commodity, Emily and Annette returned the favor and rode bikes 14 miles round trip one Saturday to visit with Earl at his house. Annette, AJ we often called her, spent Friday night at Emily's house on Crystal Lane and the next day took the bike trip to Earl's. Because it was the main form of independent transportation, both were used to riding.

"We never took one break. Who needed breaks?" said Emily.

The most comfortable ride for a passenger was on a bike rack suspended over the rear fender. Unlike the previous three methods of passenger transport, this one afforded a 4"-6" wide metal platform on which to place packages or rest one's rear end. The first two provided a 1" rounded bar. The downside of riding on the rack was that most of the weight of the bike was now towards the rear of the bike. This made the steering light and a bit hairy, especially if having to take corners on gravel roads.

"One day my young nephew was on that rack as we toured the neighborhood," said Bruce. "Things were going great until he accidentally caught his foot in the rear wheel spokes. The crash on the gravel street not only resulted in a trip to the doctor for him, but caused me to lay the bike down and experience road rash for the first time. No more eight-year-old passengers on the back of my bike."

During the summer Bruce frequently rode from Springfield to southeast Eugene, close to a 20 mile round trip to visit his older sister. His mom packed him a lunch and he pedaled off to spend the day, free from chores and parental oversight. *Independence at 14. Ah, a beautiful thing.*

"I'd leave mid-morning and come back before it got dark," Bruce explained. I'd ride from my house on West M up to Main Street, take the bridge across the river onto Franklin Blvd. and into Eugene. The hardest part of the trip was when I passed Williams' Bakery and smelled all that yeasty bread. That wasn't fair. The aroma tied my stomach in knots and made me want to eat my sack lunch on the spot."

Bruce regularly rode out to my house, some two miles away, but in so doing he combined business with pleasure. On his way to see me he stopped in at the KEED radio station on Laura Street to pick up the weekly Top Forty listings. Wofford and KEED had unique relationship. KEED was the rock and roll station for the area and Bruce was the Hamlin ASB Social Promoter. He'd make his selection of the 45s for the school to buy from those lists. He also got to watch the disk jockey behind the window spinning the 45s.

"That had to be the best job in the world, not to mention the coolest," Bruce said.

The bike was our key to transportation freedom and social networking. It would take us wherever we had the energy or desire to go. One of the clearest memories of bikes came during the summer between our 8th and 9th grade years. Bruce and I and some friends rode one afternoon through the grounds of the high school talking about what it would be like to go there and dreaming of the adventures yet to come with girls, cars, and sports. That was our future, for sure, but during those summers it was all about the bike.

Tugging on Superman's Cape

"Here comes summer. School is out, oh happy day…"
Jerry Keller, 1959

"M orning," Dad said from the dining room table where he was downing a cup of coffee and sorting through the news and mail from the previous day. "Well, Mark, what's on your schedule for the day?"

"I don't know. I haven't even thought about it," I replied. Which, in all honesty, was the truth. It was a little after 7:00 in the morning, the first day of summer vacation, June 11, 1960. I had just completed 8th grade, my first year in a public junior high. Knowing I didn't have to pack a lunch or worry about what clothes to wear, I really didn't have any plans for the day — other than grabbing a couple of pieces of cinnamon toast, some cereal, and 2-3 glasses of cold milk.

One thing that would take some of my time would be Junior State baseball, but that wouldn't start for another couple weeks. For me the month of June was slow and easy. There would be bike rides to see friends – and accidentally dropping by girls' houses to see if they were home – "we were just in the neighborhood" – bike trips to the grocery store, washing windows, or hanging laundry on the line for Mom. If Dad weighed in I could be mowing a section of our two-acre yard or pulling weeds. But just as I was brushing the toast crumbs from my mouth the phone rang. Dad walked over and picked it up.

"Yes, he is," he said and held the phone out to me. "It's for you."

"Hi, Bruce," I said. "No, just a few chores around the house this morning. Oh yeah, what'd she say?" I glanced at Dad. He held up both hands meaning I had 10 minutes. Not wanting him tuning in to the rest of the conversation, I drug the phone into the hallway bathroom and closed the door. Bruce began filling me in on several conversations he'd had with MaryAlice, Emily, and Annette the previous evening. All the girls seemed to enjoy talking to Bruce.

"Yeah, I think I can make it to the pool tonight, I just need to make sure I get all the things done around here. Let me get back to you later this afternoon. I want to call MaryAlice and work out the time, OK? So what were all the conversations about," I asked. I listened intently for the next several minutes and then there was a knock on the door.

"Time to be off," said Dad.

"Oh, God, I almost forgot," Bruce said and he launched into a quick three minute revelation. "Emily said tonight she's hoping to squeeze in on the bleachers next to – " The line went dead. Darn. Dad had yanked the plug out. I hauled the black rotary phone back to the dining room and glared. Dad hid behind his newspaper wall. Some things would never be fair.

By the start of July my daily schedule began to get a bit busier. I had summer league baseball practice several afternoons a week, and then a baseball game or two in addition to that on the weekend. My team was made up of kids from Hamlin and Springfield Jr. High. We played teams from Coburg, Drain, Thurston, McKenzie and other nearby towns.

I played catcher most of the time and sometimes right field. In the outfield there wasn't a lot of action, really. A couple of times I almost got hit by a line drive during practice because I got caught up watching a honeybee working a clover patch or became distracted by airplanes that occasionally buzzed overhead.

I liked the position of being catcher best because I was always in constant motion zipping the ball back to the pitcher or to one of the bases. God knew, I could use all the practice I could get throwing to the bases. Also, as a catcher, I liked to study the batter's stance and hitting tendencies so I could call the pitches to be thrown and hold my mitt as a target for the pitcher to throw to. Some catchers put foam rubber padding in their mitts to protect their hand. I hated that. I thought they were just wimps. I liked to feel the ball in my glove when I caught it. As a result, my left hand just below my index and middle finger was swollen for a good share of the summer, but I didn't care.

Don Pickard, a pitcher a year ahead of me from Springfield Jr. High, was the main reason for my swollen right hand. He could throw a good curve ball and a smoking fastball. He had black hair and dark eyes, but also a bit of a mean streak. His face was usually arranged in either a lopsided grin from having just pulled a prank on a teammate, or a sneer for being a recipient and vowing to get even. If there was ever a confrontation on the field, you could bet he'd be right in the middle of it somehow, shoving or swinging. The July afternoon we lost a close game to Wayne Swango's Coburg team – Pickard hated losing to the fireballer, Swango – I was taking off my gear on the team bench, mad at myself for my two costly errors.

"Nice job, Purdue. Maybe you should try throwing left handed next game." Taking his sneer with him, Pickard walked away.

A second guy on that team, Lyle Jacobs, became a good high school friend. He was another of the kids that came over from Springfield Jr. High, so I didn't know him well. It was funny how our friendship developed, though. While we were warming up one day before a game he said to me, "Mark, you know you have a bad habit that is driving me crazy."

"Yeah, and what it that, exactly?" I asked.

"You always say 'you know' after your statements."

"I do?

"Yeah, you do. And here's what I'm going to do to show you. When you talk, every time you say 'you know' I'm going to repeat it." He smiled his Cheshire cat smile.

"OK," I laughed. "Go right ahead." True to his word, that summer we spent a lot of time laughing and repeating "you knows" to each other.

"I talked to MaryAlice last night, you know," I said one afternoon.

"You know," mimicked Lyle. And so it went all summer long.

And then there was Ronnie Chase, an outfielder from my junior high. Ronnie played centerfield and, like an Australian Shepard that snags every Frisbee anyone throws, Ronnie was great at catching almost anything hit in his vicinity. Like a young pup he was bright-eyed and perky, always eager to please the coach. One summer afternoon he came to the game so wired. It was like he had just downed a truckload of espressos. His conversation was like a 33 1/3 rpm album spinning at 78. Warming up before the game with him I asked him what was going on. He told me that his dad was sitting in the stands behind home plate. This was the very first event of any kind that Ronnie's vagabond father had ever come to. Ronnie wanted so badly to make his dad proud of him.

Things didn't start well. In the third inning he dropped an easy fly ball and then, in haste, overthrew his cut off man. The opposing team scored. Later in the 7th inning Ronnie overran a simple ground ball that he would normally never miss. Trying make up for these errors when he came to the plate, he swung at almost every pitch, his face tilted to the clouds, eyes closed tight. He struck out 3 times. When we trotted off the field for last bats in the bottom of the 9th Ronnie was scheduled up. One last chance.

Brad Cooper, the quick little shortstop batting before him, drew a walk and hustled down to first base. Ronnie bounced up to the plate and dug his toes deeply into batter's box. Wound tighter than a high C piano wire, he continually twisted the bat handle as if he were trying to extract the last drop of water out of a dishrag. Unlike before, this time the gods smiled on him. He lined the first pitch thrown to him to right center field and roared around first base. Coach Lehl yelled him back to the bag. He had advanced Cooper from first to third and into scoring position. I saw him glance up to the stands with a smile so wide it looked like he had swallowed the espresso cup saucer. Then his smile crumbled as his eyes scoured the stands. His dad wasn't there. I'm not sure if we won the game or not. The look on Ronnie's face as he stood staring into the bleachers from first base is frozen in my memory. He tried so hard to wear Superman's cape that day. His dad never saw him fly.

Not So Grand Theft, Auto
(The Wofford Version)

It was one of those lazy warm summer afternoons when Mom dropped me, music man Wofford, off at MaryAlice's house. It was the kind of perfect Oregon day where a light breeze kept the heat tolerable and the sky a stunning bright blue as fluffy clouds floated away from view.

Just an hour before MaryAlice, my friend – not to be confused with girlfriend – had phoned to invite me over. We often got together on these summer days, whether it was meeting at the swimming pool, a park, or her house, just to talk. Many times I rode my bike the four miles or so to her parent's house between Springfield and Eugene. Their house was much newer and in a much more upscale neighborhood than ours.

There always seemed to be plenty to do at MaryAlice's house, but we mostly spent our time yakking and listening to the latest records in her party room. It was a detached room behind the carport and the scene of many parties during our 7th, 8th, and 9th grade years. The separation from the house provided the freedom that allowed a party full of teens to turn up the music, dance, and sometimes turn down the lights and, well…not dance.

MaryAlice and I were never about that, however. We were close friends and comfortable as just friends, knowing that our romantic designs focused on others. As friends, we spent time together pouring out our adolescent hearts, talking for hours without stopping. We shared stories of unrequited love, adolescent social protocol, and school gossip. We also compared dreams of our completion of junior high, our journey to high school, and how we might confront the unknown that lay ahead.

We were on the telephone many times a day when there was no school, each pushing our family's limits on phone time. During school days, we passed notes between classes, replacing our constant telephone calls outside school time. Her notes always came with lots of hearts, exclamation points, and a variety of colored inks. My efforts were less flamboyant, but full of good-natured teasing and junior high humor. We developed the acquired artistry of paper folding in an effort to conceal our conversations and avoid being detected during passing. *Just how small can we fold them?*

I think my parents were baffled by my relationship with MaryAlice because it was uncommon for boys and girls of that age to be as close as we were. For some unknown reason, we had both found our solace in a close friendship. My guess is that no matter how I tried to explain it, they thought she was my girlfriend. There was no indication that they ever had any idea how important we really were to each other. We were as close as "peas and carrots."

So, on that August day, I jumped out of my parents' 1959 Buick *(what fins those cars had)*, thanked Mom, and hurried through the carport to their backyard. As I rounded the corner, the sight and smell of freshly mown green grass contrasted with the brightly colored beach towels MaryAlice and her friend, Arlene Kingsbury, were lounging on. They were both sporting modest two-piece swimsuits of the day, the kind that showed some midriff, but definitely not as racy as the bikinis we leered at earlier that summer in the Beach Party movies. They were giggling, clapping, and waving their hands and arms through the routine that went with the song *Willie And The Hand Jive* as that tune wafted through the open window of the party room.

It was hugs all around, out came an extra beach towel for me, and the afternoon was washed away in a flood of teen gossip and deep discussions of critical issues like who liked who, who was breaking up, and which Philadelphia teens were getting together on American Bandstand. *Okay, it's probably time to admit that although these two were just friends, some of my adolescent hormonal needs were met in those days just spending time with girls in swim suits.*

Later, we found time to wander the neighborhood, stop by the local Beverly Park store for popsicles, followed by a surprise visit to a classmate who lived across the street. It was dinner time when we ended up back in the party room, and the two girls disappeared into the house to prepare a gourmet meal of tuna sandwiches, potato chips, and Orange Crush sodas.

After dinner, we listened to more music, tried some new dances while all the time yakking non-stop. To make our conversation more exotic, we used our nicknames, generated from the note passing. I'm sure the nicknames were to disguise our identity in the event of teacher note interception, and we probably were quite proud of our exceptional stealth. MaryAlice became Marcy, Arlene chose Jo, and I, for reasons I don't - or choose not to - remember, was Kim. Our circle of friends were also assigned these new monikers, but again, not too novel.

All these names were proudly displayed on a blackboard wall in my party room, a spare bedroom in our house that my parents let me paint with many colors and modify for dancing. We took out the carpet, painted the floor, and chose outlandish colors (for the time), for each of the other walls. That black wall also included the latest sayings and song titles.

Our time together was typical of how afternoons melted into evenings and all too soon became night. When you're 13, you don't seem to care about actual time, just about the amount of light or dark outside. After all, Marcy and Jo had important questions about certain guys we all knew, including my male perspective on their availability, what they liked, certain physical aspects, and then each girl rated the guys' "dreaminess." In turn, they gave me the inside story on a selection of girls we all knew and delighted in embarrassing me by filling in deficits in my understanding of female anatomy, secrets of the feminine hygiene mystique, and inside information on who might be attempting to enhance their budding womanhood with creative uses of Kleenex.

So, it was probably an accident when one of us discovered that it was almost 11 o'clock. We knew it was dark, but when I realized how late it was, I knew that it was time for me to leave. Telling MaryAlice that it was time for me to get home prompted her to casually mention that her parents were out of town. I then realized that I hadn't seen them all day, but it was nothing new to be with her and not run into them. We had spent quite a bit of time with them and they seemed to understand our friendship, allowing us the trust of being alone. On this night, the sudden realization of no parents presented a transportation issue for me. I had told my parents that MaryAlice's parents would bring me home. MaryAlice quickly quelled my anxiety.

"Don't worry," she calmly assured me. "Sharon is here and she'll take you home." It was a relief to know that Sharon, MaryAlice's 20-year-old college-age sister, was staying at the house while her parents were out of town. MaryAlice smiled, turned, and dipped into the house to get my transportation arranged. Arlene and I resumed our in-depth teenage discussion. After a few minutes, the party room door opened and in walked a sheepish, and somewhat shaken, MaryAlice. She took a deep breath, closed and opened her eyes, then in a quiet and somber tone gave us the bad news.

"Sharon's in bed and I don't want to wake her up. You know how mad she gets." In the past, Sharon had been prone to dismissing MaryAlice, and therefore all of us, as the immature 13-year-olds we were. In any normal situation she was not too impressed, nor reactive, to our needs. The thought of waking her for a taxi run brought images of unbridled anger, yelling, or at least consequences none of us wanted to experience. So, here we were, MaryAlice, Arlene, and I, deeply scanning our collective adolescent wisdom, utilizing our crystal-clear 13-year-old logic, and calling on our almost non-existent experience, to determine how to get me home at this time of night. I'm sure that a mature observer could have heard the brain gears grinding as we went into deep thought. Many of the most obvious solutions, like calling my parents, were avoided, being safe from our skewed logic as we pondered our options.

Then it came to us. Or I should I say it occurred to Mary-Alice. Out of that adolescent mind poured a brilliant idea. She flashed a confident smile, nodded her head, and with wide-eyed exuberance exclaimed, "We'll just borrow Sharon's car to take Randy home." The other two of us immediately lit up, nodding our heads in agreement.

"Sure, that will work great – it will be fun!" we said. *It was such an obvious and simple solution. What could go wrong?*

It is best to note at this point that Sharon's car was her pride and joy. A dark blue 1950 Ford with a white convertible top. It wasn't a hot rod, didn't have fancy paint or custom hubcaps, but it was a really "neat" car that any young person in 1959 would have loved to own. Sharon would have never – *let me add one more never* – in her wildest dreams considered letting any of us drive across town, back out of the driveway, or even sit in her "baby" without her. We were terrified of Sharon and aware of her protective attitude, but MaryAlice had already ghosted into the house and returned quite proud of herself. With a beaming smile stretching her face, eyes sparkling, she displayed the keys she had "borrowed" from the kitchen table. *It never occurred to us that we were at the point of no return. None of us seemed to have a clue that anything beyond key retrieval might actually be considered a crime.*

With a little – *and I confess, VERY little* – planning, we came to consensus that Sharon waking up would be a bad idea. So, in the driveway I cautiously opened the driver's door, reached in, placed the car in neutral, released the emergency brake. We silently pushed the Ford out of the driveway. After some manipulation of the steering wheel, we pointed the front end of the car down the street. When we reached a distance sufficiently out of hearing range, we stopped to take a breath. Our mood was somewhere between excitement and giddiness, but our collective dedication to the mission kept us on track.

Okay, now to part two of our plan. Who was going to drive? To qualify for this position, the person needed to be able to drive a car with "three on the tree." That was the "in" terminology for a standard or stick transmission with the shifter on the steering column. When asked, both girls shook their heads simultaneously and verified my suspicion that they had no clue how a standard transmission worked. So by default, I was unanimously elected as driver. We would eventually understand how this astute decision stopped short of the obvious question to follow.

It was a quick orientation to locate the ignition, start the car, pull the light switch. Now it was time for me to impress the girls with my driving skills. My driving confidence was the result of hours of moving my Dad's '55 Ford work pickup back and forth in our driveway. Since about the age of 11, he had allowed me to start the truck by myself and move it in the driveway, putting it in gear, letting out the clutch, and slowly driving from end to end, moving from one side to the other, backing up, repeating the loop over and over. Between that and some back road driving while camping, I felt that I was the master of the stick shift.

So, tackling my challenge with only a few minor jerks and grinds, I cavalierly shifted the gears, manipulated the clutch, drove on the right side of the road, stopped at intersections, and generally aced the whole driving thing. It was a beautiful sight to behold – even Sharon might have been proud of my automotive prowess. *Well, then again, maybe not.* It was only after slowly turning into my driveway, pulling to an easy stop, setting the parking brake, and opening the driver's door that the obvious finally hit us. *It did actually take that long, I'm sorry to report.*

It seemed that the imaginary light bulbs above each of our heads flashed on almost simultaneously. IF I am the driver, and IF neither of the girls can drive a stick shift, and IF they have to get the borrowed car home, how does that happen? My confidence and cocky automotive prowess suddenly shattered into shards of panic.

Once again, it was time for the same Hamlin Jr. High Adolescent Brain Trust that had devised Plan A to jump into action. *Here goes the grinding brain gears again – this time with lots of smoke out the ears. What do we do now? We're probably already in trouble. Do we tell my parents what's happening? No, we'd be in more trouble. Do we call Sharon? No, we'd be in ultimate trouble, or dead.*

I'm sure if someone could have recorded our collective facial reaction, it would have made a deer in the headlights look disinterested. Once again the considerable intellectual resource that was the three of us finally reached the conclusion that someone else besides me would have to drive the car. *An amazing flash of brilliance!*

That left us with only two possible candidates, and they both stared at me looking for the miracle of another option. After the few seconds that seemed to be an eternity, MaryAlice summoned her confidence and boldly accepted the challenge. She announced that she would be the driver du jour.

"I will drive, I can do this. Really, I've got this!" We now had been parked in the driveway just outside my parents' bedroom window for several minutes so I gave a hurried orientation. MaryAlice slid over behind the wheel. *No, the clutch is the one on the left, not the middle one. That's the brake.*

"Ah, MaryAlice. Before you try to put it in gear, you need to push the clutch all the way in."

Try as she might, Marcy's feet just wouldn't quite reach the pedals, so we moved the seat as far forward as it would go. Even then, to depress the clutch, she had to scoot to the edge of the seat like a toddler attempting to slide into the pool from a sitting position.

Fortunately, the end of our driveway angled slightly downhill into the street, so with a little push, no use of reverse was necessary. Now in the street, and from the driver's side window, I tried to simply and quickly give MaryAlice my knowledge outlining the complex relationship between the accelerator and the clutch. I'm quite confident that I did a bang up job of explaining it, but it just might have been something that took more experience than conversation.

I had her to hold the clutch in at the same time as the brake while I reached over and placed the shifter into low gear. It became evident that other aspects of the orientation would have to be quickly modified and that my extensive auto jargon was of no help, so I quickly resorted to less technical terms like "thingies" and "whatchamacallits." *Girls, geez.*

Expecting uninvited traffic at any second, my coaching transitioned into the fine art of actual clutch engagement. Before I could finish what I perceived as the best possible instructions on how to let the clutch out, the car lurched forward, bucked up and down, and the engine died. MaryAlice pushed the clutch in, turned the key, and the engine snapped back to life. I repeated my previous instructions and was amazed that no cars came along to interrupt the process. Each time the engine died, MaryAlice repositioned herself on the edge of the seat, re-started the engine, and sternly glared forward, looking even more determined.

Finally, after two or three more unsuccessful attempts, MaryAlice eased the clutch out and, with the engine still alive, crept down the street. I stood there in the middle of West L Street, watching the Ford taillights grow ever fainter. The car lumbered slowly for two blocks then turned North onto Mill Street and disappeared from my view.

It was a miracle that during the entire tutorial, my parents hadn't awakened. I quietly slid my key in the door lock, tip-toed up the stairs, got undressed, and flopped wide-eyed on my bed, fighting an overpowering sense of fear and dread. *I just know that something bad is going to come of this night.*

I'm not sure how much sleep I got, but about eight the next morning, I awoke and was surprised that I had fallen asleep at all. My mind raced for what seemed hours with scenario after scenario of impending doom. It was time to find out what had happened on their way home. After all, what if they were stopped by police, hit a tree, had the car die on the way, or, the absolute worst thing, what if Sharon woke up and found that her car was missing?

My first reaction was a realization that there had apparently been no calls to my house from the police. Secondly, Sharon hadn't called looking for MaryAlice. But, even with those positives, my mind constructed a long list of possible bad things that might have happened. Waiting late enough to think it would be okay to call, I grabbed our house phone, strung the long cord up the stairs, fell onto my bed, and rotary-dialed MaryAlice's house. *My heart was pounding.*

"Moore residence, Sharon speaking." Sharon had answered the phone. Struggling to get enough moisture in my mouth to talk, I asked for MaryAlice. The initial terror of actually speaking to Sharon then translated into a futile attempt to evaluate how upset she was by reading her voice. Mustering what seemed her usual disdain, she curtly called MaryAlice to the phone. So far I had heard no conversation about having us arrested, so the lump in my throat shrunk from baseball to walnut size, but it was still present.

After a very long minute, MaryAlice finally picked up one of the extension phones. *Yes, they actually had more than one phone.*

"Hi Bruce, I need to move to a more private place so we can talk." I just knew there was something wrong.

"So, what happened?" I asked breathlessly. After a short silence, she began laughing. *It must be nervous laughter to cover how much trouble we were in, because this wasn't funny.* She continued to laugh but finally stopped to get herself together.

"You know what you didn't show me, crazy guy?" she said.

"Show you? What do you mean? I taught you how to drive the car. What else is there?" I replied.

"I didn't know how to shift the car into different gears." *My impromptu driving class had, in fact, missed one small but critical item – shifting gears.* MaryAlice went on, her conversation interrupted by twitters of laughter.

"We went all the way home in first gear. The gears didn't become a problem until we turned the corner and I realized I didn't know what else to do. It took us quite a while to get home, but we got the car back, parked in the driveway, and put the keys back where I found them."

Apparently unfazed by their close encounter, MaryAlice and Arlene then giggled their way to bed that night. They laughed about how long it took them to get home and avoided the reality of the potential tragedy, turmoil, and trouble the episode could have caused all of us. It just didn't seem fair that I was the one who worried all night.

"I woke up this morning and Sharon and her car were gone," MaryAlice continued. "She had gone to the store and didn't say a word to me when she came home." *She had said nothing, she knew nothing, she suspected nothing.*

So on that summer night in 1959, the three of us gained knowledge, experience, and perspective. We had been presented with a situation we didn't have the resources to deal with. We did the best we could with what we had, but found out that sometimes sheer naïve luck trumps likely consequences. It also taught us that we never wanted to try anything so crazy again. No doubt about it, we didn't.

During the many years since that night this episode has amused me from time to time. I wondered several times how Sharon reacted when she finally found out about our excursion. Recently, I spoke with MaryAlice, reminded her of that night, and asked about Sharon's reaction.

With some delight, MaryAlice reported to me that she had told Sharon about that night just within the past year.

"She was shocked," MaryAlice told me, "and never had a clue that we had borrowed her Ford convertible. She seemed to be astounded that three 13-year-olds would dare do this and that she never knew or even suspected it. She didn't seem happy about it, even now".

So, it took more than 50 years, but even after all that time, Sharon was still upset about her car. See, I told you she'd get mad when she found out.

Summer Days/Summer Nights

"What a day for a daydream
What a day for a daydreamin' boy…"
John Sebastian

Other than bean picking and baseball that first summer, I didn't have a lot that I absolutely had to do, but somehow my days got filled up.

After I got out of the bean field I often had afternoons to spend as my parents and I saw fit. Once in a while it would be chores to do around the house – lawn mowing, house cleaning, grocery shopping on my bike for Mom at Safeway down the road – but then there were always days free for other things. Mostly these free times involved that well-known teenage phenomenon called "hanging out." In short, that meant going somewhere, somehow, to talk to someone. Occasionally that might involve a parent transporting me to a location and the friend's parent bringing me home, but usually it just meant riding my bike to the destination.

Luckily for me, a couple of good friends, Bruce Wofford and Suzanne Jeffries, lived only a mile or two away. Bruce, my close male confidant during those chaotic years, was always plugged into music scene in some way, shape, or form. It was always radios, records, guitars, or afternoons glued to the TV watching American Bandstand. The other friend, Suzanne, the queen bee and future calendar pin up model, had her slender fingers finely attuned to pulse of the junior high social world. In her back yard she loved to hold court, stir the cauldron of social interactions. All it ever took was a quick phone call.

"Hi, Mark. Whatcha doing? Bruce and Arlene are sitting here with me in the back yard listening to KEED, just talking. Why don't you come join us?" *Oh geez, Arlene's going to be there.* Arlene was Suzanne's personal shadow, the polar opposite of Suzanne, and always looking for a way to attach herself to any unsuspecting guy. The thing that scared me most about Arlene was that she had an agenda. I had no experience dealing with determined girls like that who didn't have the word "no" in their vocabulary. I decided to chance it. Bruce and Suzanne would save me. Wouldn't they?

"Sure, I'd love to sneak on over for a bit," I said. "Be over in a few minutes." I sprayed with Right Guard, brushed my teeth, and checked my hair. Telling Mom where I was going, I hopped on my bike and pedaled the mile or so to Suzanne's place. I found the three of them laying on beach towels in the back yard soaking up the sun and sucking down Cokes. A large bowl of barbecue potato chips sat on a nearby picnic table.

"Grab a towel and stretch out, Mark," said Suzanne. Scanning the layout of bodies, I plopped down on my towel next to Bruce. I needed the safety of a buffer space and a better view of

Suzanne. As the music from the stack of records on Suzanne's portable phonograph filtered out to us through the party room window, our conversations probed the social switchboard. In reality it amounted to a sort of verbal massage of one another's egos, especially when it came how we were viewed by the other sex.

We exhausted that topic and moved on to discuss other kids, teachers, clothes, music – whatever. Mostly we just enjoyed being in each other's company and sharing our thoughts, ideas, and fears. How would any guy at that age not like having his ego inflated or hearing a pretty girl like Suzanne admit that she was also sometimes nervous and insecure.

Other than Suzanne's back yard, the favorite places to congregate during the summer months were Willamalane Park, Snappy Service on Main Street, and Risher's Drive-In near the corner of Mohawk and K Street.

Willamalane Park was a busy place. We'd either just gather to talk about everything and nothing in the shade of one of the large trees, or we'd cluster on a bleachers just west of the uncovered, outdoor pool. The afternoon pool session ran from 1:30 to 4:30.

The nice thing about being a guy seated in the bleachers at the pool was that you got to get a good look at all the girls laying in their swimsuits on the hot cement trying to get a tan. Swimsuits were not a part of girls' attire during the school year, nor were shorts, jeans, or slacks for that matter, so this was a visual treat. Maybe not the Victoria Secret runway, but close enough. Some the girls who came to this afternoon session were here as babysitters. They often brought the kids in their charge to the wading pool or the swimming pool.

When we'd had enough sun, a short walk or bike ride from the pool would take us to Risher's six or seven blocks away. There we would cram into booths and pool our money to get a large order of fries and our individual cherry Cokes. Guys and gals smushed together joking and laughing in the middle of a summer afternoon was great fun.

The other cool thing about Risher's was that it had a juke box so we could listen to our favorite songs while we laughed and traded gossip. A quarter would get you three songs, and you could make selections and deposit quarters at a small metal box at your booth. One afternoon at Risher's I became a little desperate. We had spent all our money on eats and songs, but didn't want to leave. The music had stopped. No one else in the place was paying to keep the songs rolling. The sudden lack of support from the jukebox made me nervous. Gaps in conservation just hung there begging to be filled.

"Anybody got any gum?" I asked. Dee Howell, my pixie-like bean picking buddy, scrounged in her purse and handed me a stick of Wrigley's Juicy Fruit. I passed the yellow paper wrapper to Annette and the unwrapped gum to Earl. The silver aluminum covering I folded over and creased neatly into a stiff shaft. Once I had it like I needed, I glanced around to see if anyone was looking, and then slid it down the coin chute.

"Mark, what are you doing?" asked Emily.

"OK. Bruce give it a try," I said ignoring her question.

"What do you want to hear?" he asked, flipping the pages of the jukebox listings. Oh, here's one for you, Suzanne." Bruce punched in C-4. There was a click then *Are You Lonesome Tonight?* rolled out of the large red and silver machine.

"How many do we get for a gum wrapper?" laughed Annette.

"I don't know. Let's keep punching in selections and see what happens," I said.

"My turn," said Suzanne flipping through the pages of choices. "This one fits you, Bruce," an impish grin on her face.

"What'd you play?"

"Guess you'll just have to wait till my song is over, big boy," Suzanne teased. Then Annette leaned all the way from the end of the booth dodging Coke glasses and the French fry basket and clicked in her choice, *Does Your Chewing Gum Lose It's Flavor?* And so it continued till we'd all taken a turn, seven plays for free. As the last song was playing Emily glanced at the clock on the wall.

"Hey, you guys, Annette, Dee, and I have to get going. Mom said dinner would be ready at 5:30. We have about 15 minutes to make it home. Let me out." As we slid out I reached over and pulled the metallic gum wrapper out of the coin slot then headed for the door. Bruce, Earl, Suzanne and I headed west down K Street to Bruce's house where we would call our parents to arrange for rides home. Of course, Dee couldn't resist one parting shot.

"Hope you get all your lover's questions answered, Bruce," teased Dee.

Suzanne laughed. "Oh, I think he will. I'll help him."

A smaller, less well-known spot was a dimly lit diner known as Snappy's Service #2 located on the south side of Main Street next to Light's for Music. If we were in the up town area or wanted a quiet spot for a more intimate conversation, this was the place. It had a jukebox set up like Risher's, but with outdated songs. A person was less likely to run into a mob of friends here, and the matronly waitresses could have cared less if we were there. But you could get cokes and a huge plate of fries, our dietary staple, and talk. That was what our adolescence seemed to be focused on, talking. The "he said" "she said" thing or the "Guess who likes..." conversation starter.

If I didn't spend the afternoon with friends but stayed home to do chores, Dad would often take my brother, sister, and me somewhere as a treat when he got off work. Sometimes that was to see the Eugene Emeralds baseball team play at the old Bethel Park. He'd buy us hot dogs and popcorn and we'd keep score and talk baseball with him. One night the nine-inning game stretched into several extra innings and didn't end until almost 11 o'clock. We were tired, but Dad stopped on the way home at Cable's and bought us all giant hamburgers. With our day all used up and our bellies full, we slept soundly that night.

Other times an afternoon might be devoted to a late afternoon float down the McKenzie to fish for trout. Dad often shouted encouragement to us as we shoved corn curls in our mouth.

"Whoa, we've just arrived at that 'ol fish dining table, so get ready, you clowns." Or if we hadn't had much luck in a while he'd stand up from his rope seat at the oars and begin his plea.

"Here, fishy, fishy. Here, fishy, fishy!"

Either way, it was fun to be at the ballpark or on the river as the sun set. As dusk gently descended we'd watch moths flutter near the ballpark lights or delight in swallows skimming the river water on their downward arc to snatch insect after insect. Not a bad way to end a summer day.

The real special part of summer for us teens, however, was the night scene. We could be out later than school nights and not forced to come in because of the rain or cold or having school the next day. In neighborhoods all across town kids played hide-and-seek or kick-the-can. In my neighborhood that was usually done at our house because we had a huge yard of almost two acres. We'd stay out way past dark or till our parents made us come in.

Even then, however, our night was not over. We got to stay up later on the weekends to watch *Ed Sullivan* or *Bonanza* on TV. For some strange reason we used to forsake any chairs or couch to watch these programs. Instead we'd lie on the floor in front of our black and white Zenith propped up on our elbows snacking on bowls of popcorn. Of course, TV evenings would have never been complete without at least once hearing Warning #6 on page 37 in the Parent Manual regarding TV viewing: "Mark, you kids, move back. You're going to ruin your eyes!"

Sometimes we'd outlast Mom and Dad. They'd head off to bed allowing us to stay up really late. Once they'd left the room we'd flip over to channel 6, KOIN TV out of Portland, and watch *Portland Wrestling* with Shag Thomas, Ed Savage, and Gentleman Ed Francis. If after that no one came out to shoo us off to bed we'd turn the volume down and watch *Showtime on Six* which featured my favorite Charlie Chan or World War II movies. We knew our TV watching was done for the night when the test pattern with an Indian head flashed onto the screen and the *Star Spangled Banner* played. No more broadcasting. The station had signed off and gone to bed. We reluctantly followed suit.

If it was a week night with bean picking and baseball practice the next day, we headed to bed about 9:30 or 10:00. The house got quiet. Crickets chirped outside the bedroom window. Most teenagers, however, were busy listening to other things, most notably their trusty transistor radios.

During the daytime the station we dialed in to listen to rock and roll hits was KEED, "the nifty 1050 on your dial." Because most radio stations were sunrise to sunset stations, KEED was no longer an option at night. The station we then tuned to after dark was KASH 1600 at the very top of our AM band. It had a DJ named Dale Reed who hosted a program from 8-11 p.m. called "Top Pops."

The crowning touch, however, was to be truly lucky with a more powerful table radio. If the weather conditions were just right, you had a long enough antenna, and the radio was positioned perfectly, we could occasionally pull in the "outlaw X" stations transmitting from the Mexican border and listen to Wolfman Jack. When that happened, the world was golden. *I later read that the quarter million watts they used, illegal in the U.S., were so strong the broadcasts reportedly killed birds that flew too close to the transmitting tower and made nearby parked cars' lights glow.*

Besides playing kick-the-can till dark, watching TV, or laying in bed with our transistor radio next to our ear, we had yet a couple more after dark options. The most readily available was the swimming pool. If we wanted to be truly cool we arranged to meet friends for the more grownup evening session. Our parents would drop us off after dinner and we would stay until the pool closed at 10:00. This was too late for little kids, so teenagers dominated the crowd. The pool played rock music through its outside speakers and turned on the under-water lights to enhance the evening mood. I usually swam without a mask or goggles, and when I bobbed to the surface and looked up at the overhead lights shining down on the pool, they all had rainbow-like circles around them. If I brought or borrowed a mask I could check out all the bright and colorful swimsuits the girls wore as I practiced holding my breath while swimming underwater from one side of the pool to the other. Any way I looked at it, water was a magical medium for teenage interactions and flirtations.

The most treasured summer time event for us junior high kids was the nighttime dance under the stars at the tennis courts. It was held once a year in conjunction with the Springfield Broiler Festival in mid July. We got to listen and dance to both live music and 45s. The air was warm. A couple of distant streetlights cast conical pools of gold as the only artificial illumination. High school and junior high guys and girls from all over the city filled the three courts.

In some ways this, for us, turned out to be both a good and bad thing. It was good in that we got to talk to and get a good look at kids we seldom mixed with from the other two junior highs. It was bad in that other guys got a shot at "our" girls. As guys we didn't mind meeting girls from other schools, we just didn't want to lose our own. We found ourselves to be a bit more territorial than we were willing to admit. Maybe this was a microcosm of the real world just a few years away.

As was true with most social scenes, the girls at the dance seemed less inhibited than the guys. Once the music started on the courts the girls started twitching and found it difficult to just stand idly by. Out onto the tennis courts they'd go, dancing with each other. I always admired their spunk but never really understood the real strategy involved.

"We'd grab another girl and start dancing for a reason," Annette later told me. "I suppose we hoped you'd notice us and like what you saw. If we were successful we knew it wouldn't be long before you found your way to us. Yeah, it was sort of a deliberate tease, but if we had waited for you guys the dance would have been half over by the time you got there." I would be the first to admit their strategy worked.

"Yeah," Bruce said one night. "What's not to like about the girls we'd been chasing all school year showing up in white Bermuda shorts and those pastel tank tops." Comments then circulated about how much the girls looked a bit different than when school let out. Maybe there had been changes, but I suspect the summer outfits – swim suits, shorts, and tank tops – left much less to our fertile imaginations. I'm not sure if that was a good thing or a bad thing.

One thing I am sure of, though, was how carefree those summer months seemed, especially now. Much like that open-air pool, we were a generation that spent the long days in the sun or under the stars at night and without a wristwatch, a bike lock, or a cell phone. For me that was a good thing. A very good thing. By the way, I still don't know if Bruce – or Clyde McPhatter – ever got all their "Lover's Questions" answered. Suzanne never told me. I guess you'll have to ask Bruce.

The 58 Special

The next year our 9th grade football season was even better. We inherited an Oklahoma transfer, Russell Wadlow. He showed up at school with freckles, hair like straw dripping out of a hayloft, cowboy boots, and a lot of "y'alls" in his talk. He was surely funny to see, but a heck of a young quarterback

Two of our linemen, both tackles, bulked up during the summer after 8th grade and became defensive stoppers and offensive road graders for us backs. Luke Snider, our right tackle had what looked to be a Charles Atlas physique even at the tender age of 15: slim hips, a narrow waist, and shoulders that were measured with a yardstick, not a tape measure. Delmar Dykes, our gangly left tackle, seemed more like a grizzly than a boy when he stretched out to grab another team's runner or reached up to slap down a pass. The orange Nehi they were drinking while carrying irrigation pipe and picking beans that summer must have been their steroid of choice. Earl "The Deviant" Dwyer, my track buddy, joined us for a full season and created a deep threat in the passing game.

The game against Springfield Junior High that fall show-cased all the changes that had occurred during the summer of 1960. For the Springfield game, JC Johnson, our coach, de-signed a trick play. On our very first play from scrimmage Rus-sell Wadlow took the snap from Don Mittman, our center, and pitched the ball to Bruce Ott sweeping right. Every defensive player on the field – and a couple from the sideline, no doubt – raced up to tackle Ott. Bruce hit the brakes and abruptly heaved a pass way down field to Dwyer, the speedy receiver who had blown past the Springfield defensive backs and was all alone.

"I'll never forget that little play," claimed a grinning Dw-yer. "It was called the 58 Special. I remember seeing the look of 'Oh, crap' on the defensive back's face as we raced by each other going in opposite directions. The only problem was that Ott threw such a rainbow, the ball seemed to stay up there for-ever. I had to stop and wait for it. I was wearing glasses, if you remember. They were kind of smeared up, not real clear, and I could hear all the screaming. I caught it, somehow, thank God."

So what happened after the catch? "We scored, of course," said Wadlow, the quarterback. The words, "of course," were indicative of the team's attitude that year and of our record, a perfect 5-0!

But the best part about that season was the camaraderie and joking that went on all season long. One Monday in prac-tice Mr. Johnson asked Wadlow, our new quarterback, why he had thrown a pass instead of handing it off to a back like he was supposed to.

"Well, I got the ball and was going to hand it to Tommie, but then I looked up and all I saw was y'all so I just got rid of it." The play went for a big gain. Grinning, Mr. Johnson just shook his head while the team clapped and laughed.

That season was memorable even for my second string center-musician-crazy dancer buddy, Bruce.

"I was ticked off that Eddie Biddle got to start ahead of me, and then Don Atkinson aced me out. I was thinking that maybe football wasn't my thing. Then one game I started on the kickoff unit. I sprinted down the field as fast as my feet would take me. Hollens and I hit the returner at the same time, me low, Jerry high, and got swarmed by the team when we came off the field," said Bruce. "Probably the highlight of my short football career."

Bedroom Eyes and Bass Drums

Beginning in the fifth grade, I, Bruce Wofford, knew I would be a drummer. From the day I first picked up drum sticks and was taught how to hold them, my mom seemed to be constantly redirecting me. Incessant rhythms were tapped out on anything and everything handy, furniture, walls, pots, and, oh, yeah, somewhat reluctantly, on what I should have been using all along, my practice pad. But only as a last resort. There was an ongoing concert of songs and drum cadences running in my head, sparking my hands to replicate whatever rhythm happened to pop up. I'm sure I drove my parents absolutely crazy on a daily basis.

That fifth grade year featured my introduction to band class and later that same year, I began private guitar lessons. The guitar idea was mine, but covertly pushed by my dad. I think he dreamed of seeing me on stage at the Grand Old Opry one day, but my personal guitar dreams weren't within the realm of country music. I saw myself more like the stars of popular music and the new genre, rock and roll. But, in an effort to keep my dad happy, I was sure to keep a country lick or two handy so I could play them when he was within ear shot.

It didn't take long until my teacher, Mrs. Place, formed a band with some other beginning guitar students and called us The Silver Strings. We performed at such grand venues as local nursing homes, community meetings, and veteran's hospitals, wearing thin white shirts with full, blousy sleeves, black pants, red satin sashes, and hats with flat brims with little fuzzy balls dangling around the perimeter. We were too naïve and excited about being in a real band to be embarrassed.

My entry into junior high marked my total enmeshment in music. I discovered that my musical aptitude granted me both the penchant for learning quickly as well as supplying my passion to succeed. While I found time to incessantly play guitar in my bedroom and drum on every surface available, those sessions usually avoided the exercises assigned by my teachers and instead centered on copying popular songs I heard on the radio.

By the ninth grade, I had joined most of the specialty bands, arriving at school early for morning rehearsals, and staying after school to help our band teacher, Mr. Boehmke. At school, I was a drum guy through and through.

Bob Boehmke was a motivated music teacher and happy guy in his late-twenties. He became a favorite teacher in the school by keeping those of us in his band classes both entertained and on our toes. For the most part, he was a nice guy, but could also be a disciplinarian, complete with the infamous hack paddle possessed by many of the male teachers. The paddle was ominously displayed on the wall of his office and while seldom used, just the sight of it seemed to provide a balance of respect and decorum in the classroom.

I think the paddle was more about respect than fear, a visual reminder rather than an implied threat. Even with that caveat, "Mr. B" had a cool demeanor, punctuated by a wry smile that always made students wonder what he was thinking.

Mr. Boehmke's appearance marked him older than his true age. This was due to a horrific car crash several years earlier. One of the consequences of his trauma was premature baldness, a source of good-natured teasing. It was a safe bet that chronic pain and other physical issues were a daily challenge due to his history, but we never heard a complaint. If there were any physical problems, they didn't stop him from living his life with a positive attitude, an unbridled passion for music, and an amazing, but off-center, sense of humor.

One morning before school, my friend, Brad, and I had arrived early for Dixieland band practice. After rehearsal, we were helping Mr. B in his office. As we sorted and collated band music, the conversation got to the question we had all wondered about since we had come to know Mr. Boehmke. Whether it was courage or a dare, I don't recall, but Brad finally blurted out the hesitant inquiry.

"What happened to your arm to get that big scar, and the one on your head?" Most of us in the band had secretly whispered to each other about the many noticeable deep scars, but none of us had ever asked Mr. B the question.

He stopped shuffling through the sheet music on his desk and glanced up at us. Apparently noting our anxiety, he reassured us.

"It's okay to ask. I'll tell you". He seemed to understand just how nervous we were to directly ask him this serious question. So, in a quiet, though somber, voice, he sat back in his desk chair, stared at us, and told us the story about the car crash that almost killed him. His serious tone and demeanor forged an implied contract. He would gladly tell us once, but it would be just once.

"One night I was driving home on the interstate after a gig at a suburban club in the Portland area. It was well after 3 a.m. I was really tired, dozed off, and the next thing I knew I woke up to see the right side of my car crashing into the guardrail."

His sketchy recall included a fleeting, dream-like image of his speedometer at over 110 miles per hour. He described how that realization of speed was interrupted as the car destroyed the guardrail and wrapped around a utility pole. His voice remained low and almost sad. He looked visibly shaken, eyes straight ahead, as he recounted this incident.

At times during the story, he lamented segments of poor memory and at others he spoke of the pain that was permanently etched on his mind. His most painful detail was waking and feeling that his skin was on fire. The crash had merged the passenger and engine compartments into one, and he realized that he was lying pinned against the hot engine. That explained the burn scars.

He methodically pointed out scars, cuts, surgery sites, and burns, explaining how he had been told at various junctures that he had almost died, might never walk again, and might have a chronic debilitating brain injury. His story continued to detail long and tedious in-patient rehabilitation spanning many months.

As young teenagers, we watched with wide-eyed interest as he inventoried all the plates, pins, and screws he would carry in his body for the rest of his life. The story ended with his admission that he felt that he was a walking miracle. He was thankful just to be alive. After that morning, we never spoke with him again about that episode, but felt we were much closer to him.

The crash didn't take any of Mr. B's musical talent. He continued his career as an accomplished trumpet player, after playing professionally at an earlier age. Throughout his college years and as a full time teacher, he still found time to play music on the weekends. On occasion, he would tell stories about his younger playing days to those few of us in his inner music circle.

I realized that some of those stories might have been questionably appropriate for junior high age kids, but we incorporated them in the context of just how cool we felt he was. Our respect seemed to grow as we came to honor and share his love of music. His stories and our respect for him allowed us to accommodate his disruptive, offbeat, spontaneous humor.

One day during 4th period band class, in the middle of a particularly challenging classical piece, I was intently watching Mr. B's baton from the percussion section on the top tier of the music room. The band was finally conquering the musical piece we had been practicing. My eyes were wide open, locked on the music stand in front of me awaiting Mr. B's cue. My stare bounced up to glance at him then back to the music as I silently counted the measures, 20-2-3-4, 21-2-3-4, to make sure the tympani came in at the correct instant, even if I missed his cue.

Out of the blue, his baton clacked loudly against the music stand, signaling a stop, and after a few awkward blats and squeaks, every last instrument fell quiet. The entire band waited in uncomfortable and somewhat confused silence as we glanced about to see what might be wrong. After a significant pause, his head elevated slowly, his eyes locking directly on me. He took a breath.

"Wofford, do you know that you have bedroom eyes?" he said in a completely deadpan voice. The heat of a growing blush traveled up my neck and radiated from my face. I felt like a glowing electric heater as the first few snickers of laughter from my classmates quickly swelled into a full cascade of laughter that traveled up, down, and around the tiered levels of the band room. His "bedroom eyes" terminology confused me. I wasn't sure what that meant. I thought it must be something risqué, so I began to laugh as well. His stare continued. He waited about 15 seconds – it seemed like an hour – cracked a wry smile, and winked. Then he dropped his head, lifted his baton, and away we went. I later realized that little episode was classic Boehmke, to a T. It was just who he was,

It was not long after that episode, following an afternoon band class, that Mr. Boehmke asked me to step into his small office, just off the band room. After some relief that I wasn't in trouble, he asked me if I thought it would be okay with my parents for me to go with him to a rehearsal of The Starlighters. This was the local professional big band that performed all over Oregon. It was a huge ego boost to have been asked. I was so excited. It seemed to take forever just get out the word "yes."

So, just after six o'clock on Thursday, after clearing it with my parents, Mr. B stopped by my house in his white '58 Chevy convertible. Sliding into the passenger seat of this incredible car was the dream of a teen car lover. White exterior, red interior, and white top. As we casually cruised across Eugene to the Musician's Union Hall, many other little details impressed my 14-year-old mind.

First, it seemed so different seeing a teacher away from the usual school setting. Mr. B seemed so different, relaxed, conversational, and friendly as we cruised with the top down through Springfield and Eugene on that warm evening. Secondly, he casually smoked a couple cigarettes during the drive and it finally registered why he always smelled heavily of smoke when he first entered the band room.

Wheeling into the parking lot, we walked together down the sidewalk and entered the Musician's Union rehearsal hall. It became immediately obvious that Mr. B was very popular with the other band members. He was greeted by humorous cat calls and good-natured joking from other band members as they all unpacked their instruments. I felt a genuine familiarity, kinship, and the obvious mutual respect amongst these musicians. *Wow, how great it would be to be part of this, I thought.*

The band members were milling around, arranging their chairs, adjusting music stands, and warming up their instruments. Mr. B called me over and took the time to introduce me. Then after several introductions, he reverted to his old form.

"You people better be nice to him. You're looking at a future drummer for The Starlighters." As I scanned the musicians in the room the only person who didn't seem to find the comment funny was the band's drummer. He didn't react at all to the comment but continued to find a reason to fuss with his drum set.

As the band organized and everyone got seated, I found a chair against the wall and settled in to watch. I felt included and bursting with pride from Mr. B's introduction to the band. It was so validating that Mr. B would say such a thing about me. My smile felt wider than my face, and it seemed that I grinned so hard my cheeks ached.

Without any warning, there was a quick call from the director, a trombone player named Caleb. And, with the rustling of hand-written musical arrangements and a quick countdown, the band blasted out of the gate with *Take the A Train*. I was immediately mesmerized, smitten with the music and the performers.

From there, the band moved to *April in Paris, String of Pearls*, and then on to *Woodchopper's Ball*. That night, my life had found something very special. I was hooked on big band music. The melodies were catchy and solid, the harmonies complex and rich, the rhythms both driving and subtle. I marveled at the intricate arrangements that featured the textures of blazing brass instruments, throaty and smooth woodwinds, all within the control of the precise rhythm section.

As I sat there, my imagination put me in that drum set and I dreamed of being their drummer some day, just like Mr. B had said. I studied every move the drummer made that night and soaked in every beat. At one point, I caught myself playing drums with my hands on my thighs and, rather embarrassed, hoped no one saw me.

The exhilaration that engulfed me that night gave me thoughts of growing up in the era where big band music was common. I fantasized about conducting my own big band, running my own nightclub, or sitting in the drum set for one of the great band leaders. The wonderful gift of recognition that Mr. B gave me that night is something I never forgot.

Many times in the next few years I returned to Starlighter rehearsals, and I was fortunate to see them perform in numerous venues. I'm sad to admit that I never became their drummer, but played with other bands and still cherish every memory of live big band music. In high school, we even had a big band that traveled to play other school's proms.

To this day, the sound of that raw power, musical texture, and rich harmony still gives me pure joy – just like that first night. Both the introduction to big band music and the feeling of pride from a respected mentor were never forgotten.

I recently learned that Mr. B has passed.

Mr. Boehmke, I never had a chance to properly thank you for your wonderful gift. It is something still precious to this day.

Bass Drums

The dynamics of junior high band culture were separate from the larger school society. Many of my closest friends, like Mark and MaryAlice, weren't a part of the music experience. Many of us in the band traveled in different circles. We were vastly different outside of the musical experiences we shared. It was an "in the band – out of the band" thing. But it was a positive rather than negative.

The common bond in band gave those of us in band a unique and separate experience The music department also had activities exclusive from others in the school, from our special musical events to social activities like hayrides or parties with the choir. Because of the separate society, music was quite different from other electives like art or shop.

The respect afforded a person in the music group might vary quite noticeably from that same person's status in the larger school society. While one of us might be more popular in school society or maybe just another nerd, we all appreciated and honored each other's talent and commitment to music. As a rule, most cliques and classifications seemed to fall away at the band room door.

One of the constants in junior high society was the permeation of boy/girl dynamics and the accompanying drama. My female band interests seemed to center on the flute players. OK, and the clarinet players. Well, a certain trumpet player, too. But it was the flute players that always seemed to be the most desirable females in the band. They were in the front row, sitting in an almost stiff upright posture that accentuated their curves. I found the way they pursed their lips when they played surprisingly titillating.

I had an early crush on a girl that I knew both in and out of band. AJ was a very talented trumpet player which, being female, was a bit unusual, but like many other of my dream girls of that era, my fantasy of a romantic heart throb faded as we became good friends and energetic, but only friendly, dance partners.

The junior high years clobbered me with the reality that my future was somewhere other than athletics. I really enjoyed playing football, but neither my talent nor passion measured up to my aptitude for, and love of, music. From my first day in seventh grade band to the district honor band in the ninth grade, it seemed that whenever challenged, I moved onward and upward.

Outside of band, a short guitar performance at an all-school talent show established a new identity for me. With one song on my electric guitar, my social stock rocketed to a new level of respect and recognition, not to mention an immediate "coolness" factor.

So, between the band experience and the guitar playing, music took over my junior high life. Even the principal seemed to be a part of it. He asked me to select and buy records for school dances. This was perfect since I was a rock and roll guy and up on the latest music at the time. My band experience firmly planted my feet in all varieties of music. Such was the case with our school district's Director of Music.

Floyd Ellefson must have been in his sixties, probably late sixties or early seventies. He was a balding man that always wore a suit and tie, looking stern most of the time. He was near retirement and occasionally showed up at our band class to observe and sometimes conduct. Mr. Boehmke would also ask him to lead the band at many of our concerts and when he conducted, he always chose a march, a circus march.

Mr. Ellefson's history was unique and fascinating. As a young man he had been a trumpet player in various circus bands, mostly under the direction of Karl King. King was a prolific composer of marches in the days when every circus traveled with its own band. He became a well-known director of many smaller circus bands during the early decades of the 20th century, and even moved up to lead the Barnum and Bailey band during the teens.

At rehearsals, Mr. Ellefson would preface each march with a background story about the origin of the march, reflect on his days with a circus band, or detail remembrances of Karl King himself. We would patiently watch as his eyes lit up, opened wide, and filled with wonder. A smile would transform his face as we witnessed him travel back to the days of his youth.

Suddenly, there he was, at the circus in 1918, living a young man's dream, smelling the sawdust and popcorn, watching the elephants. Sometimes, as the pages of his memories flipped by, he would get caught up in the moment of one of his tales. His eyes would well up with tears while his voice trembled and cracked as he recounted those days past. There was not even a twitter of laughter when his emotions got the better of him.

His experience and vivid memories linked him to a special sensitivity for these circus marches. He took the time to dissect the 6/8 time signature for us and explain the feel of a 6/8 march in great detail. To him, it was all about precision of the beat and how the performance had to be "just so" to impart the true feeling of the composer, whom he usually had known those many years ago.

Each time he would stop and emphasize that the most important instrument in a circus or other marching band was the bass drum. He explain how it needed to "lift" the beat without rushing it. There were always 10 to15 minutes of bass drum stories and specific time spent working with the bass drummer. It was mandatory to get just the right feel while more than thirty other students and Mr. Boehmke sat smiling patiently during this repetitive exercise, waiting for rehearsal to continue.

With each of those tutoring sessions, he would require the bass drummer to play by themselves while he critiqued their timing amid excited shouts and grand arm gestures. The bass drum part was nothing more than single notes on the beat, but he insisted that the entire march be played while he voiced the melody.

It was embarrassing to be the one in the spotlight, but if I was the lucky drummer subjected to the "clinic," I willingly performed just as he asked. As redundant as it might have seemed at the time, I think we all really enjoyed being a part of his return to those golden days and watching him glow in the memories.

Those sessions were a firebrand test to our limited adolescent patience, but we all took a breath, relaxed, and gave him the stage.

To this day a spontaneous smile draws across my face when I hear a 6/8 march that Mr. Ellefson might have conducted. I listen closely and pay special attention to the bass drum. It's the most important instrument in the marching band.

Almost X-Rated

There were always experiments and firsts, but not necessarily the kind any self-conscious 13-year old looked forward to. Almost anyone who has survived being a teenager probably has had the misfortune to have experienced or witnessed some of the following.

One day Jay, a slow learning 7th grade boy, was competing with a group in his social studies class against another team as part of a review for an upcoming test. The score between the two teams was tied. Jay rotated to the front of the line for his team, his eyes wide, anxious to score the go-ahead point.

"What is the name of the large river in Egypt that flows north into the Mediterranean Sea?" asked the teacher.

"The Tigris?" said Jay awaiting the teacher's response.

"No, you idiot," blurted a teammate. Jay deflated as if he'd been gut-punched. He retreated to a desk at the end of the line. His hands covered his face. A few minutes later the teams' cheers and groans over student responses to the teacher's questions were overcome by the sound of sobbing from a back corner of the room. A panicked look spread across the class. Several girls and boys rushed from their desks to comfort Jay who was slumped on the floor. They repeatedly reassured him that "everything was OK" and that "they were so sorry." The teacher abruptly ended the contest. Jay wasn't at school the next day.

Of course, there were always a few students who felt no sorrow for the victims of their pranks. To make matters worse, they then pretended to be clueless as to why they should find themselves in the principal's office. Chuck Foret, a bow-legged 8th grader who actually needed to shave daily, was one of those.

"OK, I did it," admitted Chuck. Mr. Hayden and Mr. Rose shook their heads. "What's the big deal? No one was hurt. It was all in fun." What Chuck had done was walk up behind Stewie, a special ed student, with a pair of scissors and snip his suspenders. Stewart, angry and embarrassed, ran to the office to report the incident.

Other times the joking and teasing was less vicious, but embarrassing nonetheless. Junior high was bad enough if you screwed up without anyone noticing, but mortifying if you messed up in front of a crowd.

One Tuesday morning I approached a group of 8th grade girls huddled in the breezeway between classes. They all seemed to be ribbing a classmate in the center of their circle. I slowed to see what was going on.

"Wahoo, next time, Sherri, let's hope you'll remember to bring your 'big girl' money." Two quarters sailed through the air and fell to the breezeway cement by Sherri's feet. The girls ran off laughing, leaving Sherri standing alone, the object of stares and whispered conversations. I didn't understand the comment at the time.

The guys weren't any better. Seated with some of my 8th grade teammates one afternoon in the bleachers of the large gym waiting for our coach to appear to start basketball practice Lonnie Poole, a knuckle-dragging 9th grade team member, approached us.

"Hey, you know that if you play with yourself your palm turns yellow?" he said. I stared at him trying to figure out if he had just said what I thought he'd said. Here I was just a few months out of Sister Martha Mary's jurisdiction at St. Aloysius and I got a comment like this lobbed my way. Nervously rolling my eyeballs to the left and right I saw a couple guys staring down at their upturned hands. Lonnie thrust his index finger at us. A gigantic grin spread across his pimpled face.

"Gotcha," he crowed then turned and trotted off to join his buddies at the far end of the gym.

The Peeping Tom

Our questionable junior high humor regularly teetered on the precarious edge of acceptability. For instance, there was the standard group attempt by girls, amid a chorus of shrieking and laughing, to push another girl into the guys' locker room. Balancing the idiocy was the loudmouthed showoff guy opening the girls' dressing room door and yelling, "Close your eyes, girls, I'm coming in." That testing of the limits and stretching of the lines of the appropriate was regularly on display. The girls usually just laughed about the pranks, as did the boys. Laughter often masked nervousness and uncertainty.

Then there was the spring day when the laughter wasn't funny any longer.

DJ Canon, a wiry blond 9th grade athlete, let his hormones run unleashed one Friday afternoon. As a last period PE helper DJ was responsible for shuttling archery equipment from the storage room out to the huge grass field behind the large gym. Once everything was set up for the coed class, he and the female PE helper floated around assisting students wherever needed.

Being a PE helper was definitely considered a plum job reserved for trustworthy kids. On this particularly warm spring day, after the students had finished their target shooting, they were told to take two laps around the track before heading in to shower. While the classes were circling the track DJ and Serena, the female PE helper, gathered all the targets, arrows, and bows and stacked them on a cart which they towed to just outside the storage room. As the PE instructors followed the last of their plodders into their respective locker rooms to monitor behavior, DJ made Serena an offer.

"Hey, Serena, I can get this today. Go ahead and take off. I'll lock up." She thanked him and hurried away. Quickly DJ began stuffing the archery gear in the storage room. As he lifted the last target bale up towards the top of the stack DJ's eyes noticed a blur of gray scuttle along the top of a pile of targets to his right. He let go of the bale in his hands.

"You'd better run, you worthless little furball," he mumbled. Then snatching the bale again he looked toward the ceiling. "What the heck," he said. "Is that your hiding place. Mr. Mouse?"

Crawling up to investigate, DJ peered cautiously at a quarter-sized hole for a few seconds, halfway expecting another gray blur to rocket out. When it didn't, he leaned in closer and got another shock. Instead of the cavity of the wall being dark, light streamed out as if the mouse had left its living room light on.

DJ stuck his forehead against the wall, his right eye right up against the hole. Peering into the opening, his whole body snapped rigid, muscles taught, his breathing almost silent. After five minutes of being glued to the hole, he silently crawled down, grabbed the bale he had dropped and tossed it to the top of the stack. The hole was again covered up. DJ reached the handle of the storage room door behind him, opened it quickly, and slipped out into the sunlight. Grabbing his school clothes from his PE locker, he raced to catch his bus ride home.

Typical of Oregon's spring weather, the next Monday a chilly rain descended on the valley. Rotating through my morning classes it struck me as a bit odd that DJ was not in my 3rd period shop class. In fact, I couldn't recall him getting on the bus that morning. I turned to Derek Macklin, the boy working on the lathe next to me, and asked if he knew where Canon was. Derek, a close friend of DJ's, was a well-dressed daredevil always up for the next wild adventure. His family owned the bowling alley in town and they lived around the corner from the Canons.

"I'm not real sure," Derek said. "I saw him Saturday at the hardware store. He was having a key made for a lock. Said he'd lost his house key and wanted to make sure he didn't get locked out again. He seemed all right to me then. Maybe he got sick or something. I'll check on him this afternoon when I get home."

I got through the rest of the day, but due to the rain, PE was moved indoors. We played indoor dodge ball. This kind of put a damper on the day. I missed being outside. On the way home on the activity bus Bruce, Earl, and I began discussing the upcoming Friday night party at Suzanne Jeffries' house. We wondered who Suzanne might pick to fill in for DJ if he was still sick.

"He isn't sick," said Jack Birksey, from the seat behind us. Jack was a social creature who seemed to be able to keep track of the movements of many classmates. "I saw him locking up the storage room after 7th period today. Not sure what JC had him put in there, but I'm pretty sure it was DJ I saw coming out."

About a week later a few of the pieces to this strange puzzle snapped into place. DJ approached me in the breezeway after 3rd period. He slid four 5 x 7 black and white pictures out of a large manila envelope.

"Hey, hey, hey," he began obviously impressed with himself. "Whaddya think of these babes?" He flipped through the pictures slowly. I locked up as I took in three 9th grade girls, all of whom I knew well, stepping unawares from their PE showers. He saved his trump card for last. It was a picture of Lisa Aldridge, my girlfriend at the time. My insides tightened like the rubber band on a balsa glider.

"DJ, give me that picture!" I said through clenched teeth. He looked right at me. A slow grin worked its way across his face. DJ continued to twirl the propeller.

"Nah, I think I'll just hang onto it a while and see if other guys might like to have a peek."

"Dammit, DJ, this isn't funny. Give it to me." While he was taller and stronger than me, I was gambling that he wouldn't want to cause a scene in the breezeway within earshot of the principal's office during passing time. Too many witnesses. I wasn't thinking of what might happen to me. What was flashing across my mind was how Lisa would feel like having her picture paraded around in front of so many leering eyes, not to say anything of the other girls whose pictures were in that envelope.

"OK, OK. Take it easy, Mark. Just kidding," he said trying to end the unexpected confrontation. He thrust the picture of Lisa at me and then ran off to class to beat the tardy bell. I stuffed the picture into the back of my notebook and hurried to class, the notebook trapped tightly against my side. At lunch I told Bruce and Earl what had happened.

"What are you going to do about this, Mark?" Bruce asked.

"I'm not sure. Think we should tell the girls? Or would it be better to go to Mr. Rose?"

"You mean Saul T, our principal?" mocked Earl. "Forget that. Personally I'd like to beat the snot out of that pervert and just take his snapshots."

We talked anxiously about what we could do to grab the pictures before they circulated any further. Before we could form a plan the bell rang sending us off to afternoon classes.

Throughout the rest of that day I kept my notebook clamped shut, only yanking out sheets of paper for classwork from the front, never risking opening the notebook the whole way. It wasn't until I got home and was alone in my bedroom that night that I extracted the print and stared at it. Anger boiled to the surface again. Then without thinking any further,

I ripped it into small pieces, carried it to the living room, and pitched it into the fireplace flames. Two days later DJ got called into the principal's office.

Obviously the cockiness over his deed had overshadowed his fear of being discovered. I'm not sure what happened to him because of what he did or how many kids ever knew that the picture taking had occurred. I never told Lisa about it. It was such a unsettling event during that 9th grade spring. I was embarrassed for her and didn't want her to know. These girls weren't Playboy models flippantly posing for a camera. My initial anger was for them. Part of that was the feeling that somehow I, too, had been violated. Lisa was an important part of my life at that time. And DJ? Although we continued to play on the same sports teams together for the next three years, things were never the same.

The Break In

In the '50s and '60s school was organized into two parts: elementary (grades 1-6) and secondary (grades 7-12). In the first six years students learned basic information and rules of social conduct and appropriate behavior. In the last six years, much to the frustration of their parents, students experimented with stretching or breaking a lot of those rules.

It was during junior high, the first three years of that secondary education, that experimentation really began. Natural curiosity, social pressure to try new things, the desire to fit in and be accepted or noticed, all began exerting its influence.

"During that time there were so many firsts," Annette Jensen recalled. "Everything seemed so exciting." Kids tried out for sports teams and either made it or got cut. Kids ran for student council, Girls League, Boys Alliance, and rally squad. The student body, like Romans holding thumbs up or down for the gladiators, voted to determine the winners and losers of those popularity contests. Cliques, couples, and friendships were formed and broken. Along the roller coaster ride of junior high experimentation a person could secure attention in socially acceptable ways, or they could make a name for themselves in a different way.

On a chilly Friday night in October of 1960 Jim Tracey, Buddy Collins and Delbert Cotzler decided to nudge the limits, to get a rush that school hadn't provided. Inching along the inky south wall of the old Holland Market they reached the back door of the refrigerated storage room. Del, gritting his teeth, slowly twisted the knob and then threw a silent shoulder into the old wooden barrier. It opened easily.

"See, just like Terry said. They rarely check to make sure it's locked,'" Del whispered. "Let's go." Flipping on a flashlight Tracey quickly located their target. Then he switched it off, and the young thieves each lugged three cases of beer out into the nearby orchard. Del slipped back and closed the door. It was eerily quiet. At 2:00 in the morning no traffic moved along the country road in front of the old market.

"I'll get the car. You guys stay right here and keep down." With that advice, Del cut across the orchard to a dirt road where his uncle's 1950 Plymouth station wagon waited. Getting behind the wheel, he started up the old wreck and, without turning on the lights, drove out to 19th Street, then around a corner and into the empty market parking lot. Glancing around to make sure no one was watching, he inched the Plymouth past the rear loading dock to the edge of the orchard. Del left the car idling and trunk open, and jogged to where Jim and Buddy were waiting.

"Let's go. Let's go," Del urged. Tossing the cases of stubbies into the back of the car, Jim and Buddy leapt into the rear seat then silently closed the doors. The old Plymouth rolled out of the lot. Del flicked on the headlights.

"I hope we don't run into any cops in the next five minutes. We've just got to make it to the river then home." Poking along at barely 30 mph they reached Harvest Lane without encountering any traffic and hung a sharp right. About 100 yards down the lane Del once again switched off his headlights. The full moon gave him plenty of light to see his destination just a couple minutes away. When he got near the river he shut off the car.

"Grab the beer and follow me," he said. Obediently Tracey and Collins lugged the cases down the side of a big ditch to a small side branch of the river.

"Take those bottles out of the box and hand them to me one at a time. And be careful. We don't want to break any. It'll mean less beer for us."

Jim and Buddy watched as Del took one bottle after another and carefully submerged each of them in a rock-lined hole in the frigid river water. Then he covered the hole with rocks and a large tree branch. Turning, he handed each of them an ice-cold beer.

"What do you say, guys? One for the road?" A satisfied smile creased Del's face. They quickly guzzled a sample of their treasure then crawled back into the old blue Plymouth and cruised unnoticed to Del's house and a few hours sleep.

The following Monday morning the young trio headed to their first period classes, a spring in their step, a smug smile on each of their faces. By second period the smiles had begun to dissolve. A black and white Springfield police car sat in the first row visitor slot of the parking lot. Del became aware of a steady parade of boys entering and exiting the principal's office. Buddy caught up with him just outside 3rd period shop class.

"Man, I got called into the office and a cop asked me tons of questions. He wanted to know where I was Friday night and if I'd heard anything about a break-in at the market. Of course, I played it dumb. Said I had spent the night at your house watching TV. And, no, no one had told me anything about a break-in. Watch yourself. You'll probably be in there soon."

"Don't worry," Del replied. "I haven't said anything to anyone and I'm not going to. If you see Jim tell him to keep his mouth shut, you hear me." By lunch time the story was all over the school, and not long after that it became apparent that someone had cracked. Parents were notified and angry. Cotzler, Tracey and Collins' were permanently grounded and made to publicly apologize to the market manager. They also had to pay for the things that they had stolen and were banned from the store for the rest of the year.

"It was such a stupid thing," Buddy said one day in shop class. "I can't think of what prompted us to do it. I'd never been in trouble like that. I guess it was just the challenge of breaking a law and seeing if we could get away with it. I felt like such a punk and so ashamed for how I had hurt and embarrassed my folks. I'm never telling anyone. I don't want them to know."

I never felt the need to tell anyone what Buddy had told me that day. It was a time he obviously wished had never happened. When I thought about it, I realized there were times we didn't get do-overs for our mistakes or screw ups.

Who's On First?

Abbott: Strange as it may seem, they give ball players nowadays very peculiar names.

Costello: Funny names?

Abbott: Nicknames, nicknames. Now, on the St. Louis team we have Who's on first, What's on second, I Don't Know is on third.

Costello: That's what I want to find out. I want you to tell me the names of the fellows on the St. Louis team.

Abbott: I'm telling you. Who's on first. What's on second. I Don't Know is on third

Costello: You know the fellows' names?

Abbott: Yes.

Costello: Well, then who's playing first?

Abbott: Yes.

Costello: I mean the fellow's name on first base.

Abbott: Who.

Costello: The fellow playing first base.

Abbott: Who.

Costello: The guy on first base.

Abbott: Who is on first.

Costello: Well, what are you askin' me for?

Abbott: I'm not asking you – I'm telling you. Who is on first.

Costello: I'm asking you – who's on first?

Y ou can pick me up right here a little after 10," I told Dad
 through the open station wagon window. He smiled and
nodded.

"Have a good time," he said, then pulled away from the
Hamlin Jr. High parking lot. I headed down the sidewalk toward the school cafeteria. The setting sun of early October
splashed a brilliant red across the edges of the clouds to the
west. "Red at night, sailors' delight" I remembered Dad saying
to me. I wondered if those skies could be an omen. As I scanned
the milling crowd 50 yards in front of me I caught sight of Wofford and Dwyer waving just outside the open cafeteria door
and anxiously increased my pace. I joined my friends, and we
scrunched through the doors flashing our student body cards
to the teachers staffing the entrance tables. Once past the tables
we headed to the coat check station by the stage at the far end
of the gym.

Pregame Warm Ups

M usic was pouring out of speakers in the four corners of
 the gym, but no one was dancing. It was early. Like a
baseball game, the umpire hadn't yelled "play ball" to start the
game. The players were just filing onto the field loosening up.
Infield practice hadn't even taken place. In the cafeteria small
groups of students ringed the floor meshing into a shape like
the cell wall of a giant amoeba. They chatted with other groups
floating by. Although conversations, jokes, and playful ban-
ter dominated the cafeteria activity, most students were at the
same time busy with another activity – scoping out the crowd
for friends and desirable dance partners. I had spotted my favorite group of girls and marked what they were wearing. An-

nette, the talkative brunette, stood out in the dim cafeteria like a lighthouse beacon. Across the top of her head she had worn a stretchy white headband. It matched her long-sleeved white blouse and complimented the box-pleated tartan-plaid wool skirt that hung to the top of her knees. Six other girls clustered around that headband.

Infield Practice

Thirty minutes into the evening, and no one had braved taking the floor. Groups of girls shifted uneasily to the music while the boys ratcheted up their courage. Someone had to break the ice. We didn't want to stand the whole evening on this side of the cafeteria repeating the same stupid jokes and one-liners.

"Let's go ask someone to dance," I suggested to Bruce and Earl, not that I was going to be the first.

"I'll go if you will. Who you going to ask?" Wofford said.

"I don't know," I said, "but this is stupid." Dwyer, standing to my right, threw out a challenge.

"Here's the deal. Next fast dance we all walk across and grab someone. I'm asking Annette. The rest of you are on your own, but I've got Tex." We had continually ribbed Annette, the cute tomboy with freckles and a ponytail, about being a cowpoke because she lived outside the city limits and had a horse.

"OK, next fast dance. Let's do it. I'm asking Suzanne," I said.

"I'll take Emily," Bruce decided. We hoped they'd take us up on our offer. A real strike out to start things off would be humiliating. As if the teacher playing the 45s had heard our conversation, the next song out of the speakers was a guitar driven favorite, *Walk, Don't Run* by The Ventures. Being quick on his feet, Earl shot from the edge of the dance floor and headed briskly toward his target. Bruce and I hurried to catch up. Out of the corner of my eye I could see we had started something. Behind us came first one small wave of guys followed by another and then another. In front of us the group of girls we were headed for began whispering in each other's ears, giggling, and shifting positions. I was dying to know what they were saying. On second thought, maybe I didn't want to know. I felt like we were serving up our egos on a silver platter. And, of course, everyone in the gym was watching. We finally reached our destination.

"Do you want to dance?" Earl asked Annette. Bruce and I repeated the question. All three girls smiled. As we turned and headed to the center of the floor I caught secretive little glances being exchanged. *Oh, I'd give anything to be able to read their minds right now.* The girls trailed along behind us, no doubt giggling. Were we that inept already?

When we reached an opening near the center of the floor we turned, grabbed our partners' hands, and bumped along to the pounding guitar sounds. It felt good to move, stretch, get the kinks out. At the end of the song we thanked the girls and were just about to head to the sidelines when a familiar set of lyrics halted our retreat:

> *Ah, I should have known it from the very start*
> *This girl will leave me with a broken heart*
> *Now listen people what I'm telling you*
> *Stay away from a-Runaround Sue*

I was warmed up now. My legs were twitching. I wanted to dance. Isn't that why all of us had come here tonight? Well, that was part of my reason, anyway. We looked at the girls. The girls looked at us. Before anyone had a chance to say anything I grabbed Annette's hand and the six of us just picked up where we had left off 30 seconds ago, all with different partners.

"Hey," what're you chewing?" Annette asked me. "It smells good."

"Cloves. You know those spiky things they stick in hams. Mom sometimes pops them in her mouth and her breath smells good. Thought I'd try them. I was hoping to not repel any girls tonight with bad breath." Anything to improve my questionable chances, but I wasn't going to tell her that. As our little group swished back and forth we laughed and hurled wise cracks to fill the nervous void. We mouthed the words of the song we had committed to memory. The ball was rolling now.

The Early Innings

The dancing game moved along smoothly and by the end of the first hour all three grades, 7th, 8th and 9th, had claimed a section of the floor for their respective class. Sensing that a change of pace was needed, the DJ slipped on the first slow song, a plaintive Brenda Lee request.

...Alone, just my lonely heart knows how
I want to be wanted...

I looked at all the non-dancers, the wallflowers standing around the edges staring out at the paired up couples. My stomach twisted. I knew that feeling. I didn't want to admit the honesty in those lyrics. That was another reason most of us in that room had shown up tonight. But before long even the most self-conscious boys had gotten got caught up in the words and the opportunity it presented. The numbers on the dance floor swelled. It must have seemed much less challenging to hold onto a girl's hand and simply take baby steps in a small circle. When the song finished the couples began to part. Only a few seconds into the separation the DJ shouted, "Two in a row." The slow tick-tock rhythm of another slow dance allowed couples to pair up for required touching again.

As I lie awake resting from the day
I can hear the clock passing time away
Oh, I couldn't sleep for on my mind
Was the image of a girl I hope to find...

Glancing around the dance floor it became obvious the Boys' Manual for Slow Dance Behavior had not been handed out. There were couples with enough space in their embrace to insert a bowling ball and others whose technique resembled the adhesion one sees in a peanut butter sandwich. But couples were giving it their best shot. Sensing that maybe it was time to usher in a different mood the DJ chose a piano-pounding favorite:

Oh I know a cat name Way Down Willie
Got a little chick name Rocking Millie
He can walk and stroll and Susie Q
And do that crazy hand jive, too...

Many of the previously idle onlookers waded onto the dance floor to join their friends. This selection had no prerequisites in order to participate: no footwork, no knowledge, and no partner. It was the teenage version of the Bunny Hop. You could just throw your arms around in time to the music by yourself or in any kind of group. The experience was like a Bo Diddly group hug. And with more kids participating in the dancing and more pairings being attempted, the temperature inside the cafeteria began to rise. So did the expectations.

The Top of the 5th

It was approaching 8:30, halfway through the dance. Dwyer, Wofford and I had danced with most of the girls we wanted to. It was time to narrow the number of possibilities. I had played the field, but felt I needed to step up to the plate and be more aggressive, be alert to the flirtatious invitations the opposite sex might be flashing. My sidekicks felt the same. Earl had zeroed in on Lana, Junia and Annette. Bruce was pursuing Charlotte, Connie, and Norma. I had dismissed Suzanne. She, it appeared, had both her eyes on Jerry, so that was a dead end. Instead I settled on Annie, Emily, and Vicki. All of our selected girls laughed at our jokes and loved to dance – no wallflowers there. They made us feel good being around them.

It wasn't long before our dancing shoes were hard at it again. Wofford, the one who had accompanied me on my "first kiss" episode, loved to dance. When he did it was like his joints were connected by rubber bands and every other part of him, even his eyebrows, shook. He had a thing for music. He just felt it. When the hand jive song finally ended, the crowd that had gathered to watch him whistled and applauded his efforts.

But it wasn't over. Out of the loudspeakers boomed more of that twitchingly seductive music. Like a marionette controlled by invisible strings, Bruce began to move. He hit the floor with Charlotte. Earl and I followed with Lana and Annie. Gary U.S. Bonds was providing the invitation to get a little crazy.

Don't you know that I danced.
I danced till a quarter till three…

We might have dreamed of dancing till the early hours of the morning, but when the song was over we retreated to the edge of the floor to catch our breath. Bruce was perspiring heavily but grinning from ear to ear. Kids were whooping and slapping him on the back, having enjoyed watching him put his Old Spice deodorant to the test.

"You know, Bruce," an adult voice chimed from behind us, "if you worked as hard at football as you do at dancing, you'd be an All-American!" The teasing voice had come from our PE teacher and 9th grade football coach. We all laughed. Mr. Johnson flashed a grin and moved on. A slow song filtered out into cafeteria and things got more serious. I headed for #2 on my list, Emily, a petite brunette with soft brown eyes. She was wearing a full cotton skirt, white blouse, and apple-red cardigan sweater. Once on the floor I gently grasped her right hand in my left and placed my other palm in the center of her back. She looked straight at me for a full second, then glanced away. We began to move to the words.

A thousand stars in the sky like the stars in your eyes…

I struggled for something to say, but nothing came to mind. My hands began to get moist. I sensed her left hand resting lightly on top my shoulder. My right hand caught the bumps of her spine and then a horizontal band – I gulped and dropped my hand to the small of her back. My mind was racing, but my mental transmission was stuck in neutral. My id and ego were having a serious battle. *Go for it, you weenie. No, don't push your luck, you might blow it. Be a gentleman.* Following an ingrained St. Al's script, I played it safe and did nothing.

...You're with me tonight, I'm captured by your charms
Oh, pretty baby won't you hold me in your arms...

The song ended. As we released, our eyes locked again then hers darted away.

"Thank you," I said. She smiled and turned to head back to her group. Not sure of what had just happened, I stuffed my hands in my pockets and headed back to get support and advice from my buddies. I was also curious to know how they had fared.

7th Inning Stretch

Nine o'clock. One hour to go. There was a short pause in the action as the DJ announced that he would be taking requests for the last 45 minutes of the dance, and suggested that while he was compiling a list we could get some fresh air and drink of water. He'd be back spinning platters in 15 minutes. Bruce and I headed for the line at the drinking fountain. A few minutes later Earl joined us. I glanced toward the DJ and saw Annette and her circle of friends hand him a small slip of paper.

9th and Final Inning

From the outside breezeway where we'd been cooling off, we heard the music start up again. Reentering through the cafeteria door I felt two hands on my back pushing me onto the dance floor. I turned around.

"May I have this dance, Mark?" Annette asked as she curtsied mockingly.

"Anything for you," I grinned. We headed into the mob.

I love Corinna, tell the world I do
I love Corinna , tell the world I do
I pray at night she'd like to love me too...

About a minute into the dance as we pulled each other through an underarm loop AJ whispered, "Are you going to ask Emily to dance again?" I gave her a puzzled look.

"I guess so," I mumbled. Nothing more was said. We finished out the dance. Annette left smiling. A funny feeling came over me. Something was going on, but I didn't know what. I nervously waited for the other shoe to drop. It didn't take long. A girl in AJ's group shrieked as eight slow measures of individually picked electric guitar notes reverberated across the dance floor. Not knowing what the shriek was all about but recognizing this as a slow dance, I found myself in a wave of guys rolling across the floor towards all the skirts and blouses clustered on the other side. When we got there I asked Emily to dance. Arms snugged to her sides and almost rigid, she looked as if someone had just dropped an ice cube down the back of her blouse. She squirmed through a group of girls to join me.

"This is my favorite song!" she beamed bouncing up and down. As she turned to face me, the light from the music closet where the DJ was selecting the next 45 to play caught in her eyes. We got positioned and slid into the rhythm.

It's just like heaven
Being here with you
You're like an angel
Too good to be true...

We spun slowly into a circle like a leaf spiraling down from a tall maple tree. I pulled Emily closer. Our cheeks met and our bodies fused. No chance of a bowling ball getting through here. I inhaled the fresh scent of floral shampoo and a hint of some kind of perfume. It wasn't like my Dial soap bar. This was girl stuff. Moving only my eyeballs I surveyed the dance floor and noticed that Bruce and Charlotte and Earl and AJ had developed a similar pose, that of a dampened S&H Green Stamps freshly pressed onto a booklet page. This was, indeed, feeling as the song said, "too good to be true." Earl smiled at me. Bruce couldn't. His eyes were closed.

When you are near me,
My heart skips a beat
I can hardly stand on
My own two feet...

We peeled apart at the end of the song and I thanked her. Feeling like superman I asked, "Save the last dance for me?"

Flashing a grin she said, "If you're lucky." *Girls can be so unsettling at times. Do they really delight in playing with a guy's feelings?*

A fast dance played next, Jimmy Jones's *Good Timing.* I smiled to myself at the selection and walked along the bodies at the edge of the floor reliving the last four minutes. I needed time to recuperate. I couldn't figure out what had happened to my buddies, but it didn't matter. I had other things to think about. The DJ announced that the next record would be the last dance, and just like that came a favorite instrumental, Percy Faith's *Theme From a Summer Place.* I approached my petite dark-haired dancing mate.

"Am I lucky?" I asked smiling at her. She smiled. No words. I didn't need any. Actions had spoken far louder than words for this loopy 14-year old boy. We held each other and just listened to the instruments speak. It was nice to have no distractions, to just go slow and spin around in our own magic world before we separated and walked off into the night.

Fifteen minutes later I crawled into the old station wagon for my ride home. Dad turned to me.

"So, how was it? Did you enjoy yourself?"

"Yeah," I said. "It was good." Replaying the evening in my head on the ride home I didn't think I had done too badly. I hadn't struck out with anyone I cared about. I wasn't really sure if I had gotten any hits, but I felt I could now answer Lou Costello's question. I had been lucky. I think that night I had gotten to first base. I wasn't sure what was on second.

Having spent more than 30 years teaching in the world of the adolescent, I have seen nights like this many, many times. Boys and girls 13-15 years old showing up at dances in hopes of making new friends and getting to first base with someone of the opposite sex. It was then, and is now, what this age is so consumed with. They come now as we did then, seeking validation that they have been accepted and are worthwhile individuals that are admired and desired by others. Sadly, I have experienced and witnessed the frustration and seen the tears of rejection. It is part of the game. What still amazes me some 50+ years after this night at Hamlin, is that even knowing the possibility of failure, kids are still willing to put themselves out there, to risk it all. The rewards are worth the risk. There is nothing like that feeling of getting a hit your first time.

The Celtic Loggers

Our final year as Hamlin Loggers, the entire 8th grade team and 17 more guys returned to the Boys' Gym for basketball tryouts. Everything for the '61 season was different, however. We had a different coach, J.C. Johnson, and we were now playing in "the big gym." Instead of our home base being the asbestos tiled cafeteria/Girls' Gym, we got to play on the maple parquet floor with fancy pull out seating.

Our uniforms still featured the Kelly green and white colors, but there was an eerie connection in my head to another basketball team whose colors were also Kelly green and white and who played on a maple parquet floor. That was the team I raced home from church on Sundays to watch, the storied Boston Celtics.

I don't think there was ever a team that could, even to this day, generate the excitement for me that the team of Russell, Heinsohn, Cousy, Sharman, Ramsay, and the Jones boys, KC and Sam, could. On their storied team they had an all-American from the University of Oregon, "Jungle" Jim Loscutoff, a

6'8" gorilla of a forward who could bang in the paint with the brutes and also arc in long one- handed push shots.

He was a crowd favorite, a sort of rugged teddy bear. One Sunday afternoon in Boston Garden he flashed that charisma. During a contested breakaway layup by a Philadelphia 76er, a violent collision at the basket resulted in the steel pipe supports for the glass backboard getting separated. At first one of the referees tried putting the dangling pipe back into its housing. No luck. The second referee walked over to help him. Still, four hands and two bodies just couldn't get things back together. The crowd began chanting, "Loscutoff, Loscutoff, Loscutoff," and the brawny player with the pool table-like flat top stood up from his seat on the bench and began slowly ambling toward the metal wreckage, taking his good sweet time, working the crowd.

Once there, he analyzed the situation a bit, then spread his feet apart into a solid base, grabbed the dangling pipe in his meaty paws, and inserted it back into its proper location. The crowd roared its approval. Smiling, he strode slowly to center court, raised his arms into the air, and rotating, bowed in turn to all four sides of the court. Then he sauntered back to his spot on the bench and sat down.

Our 9th grade team that year also had dreams of being champions just like the Celtics. Coach Johnson had an idea how that might happen. This became clear on our first practice after the team cuts had been made.

"On the line," the coach barked. Dwyer verbalized what the rest of us were thinking.

"God, I dread those words," he said. The coach believed that in addition to any talent we might have enjoyed, the key to our success lay in teaching excellent fundamentals and in being in better condition than our opponents, being able to run faster and longer than anyone else would want to. Every day at the end of practice we did our conditioning drills. Besides the standard wind sprints, we did "lines," "duck walks," "frog jumps," and the dreaded "killers."

"Those duck walks and frog jumps should be outlawed," moaned Bruce Ott, slumped on a bench in the locker room after that practice. Bruce was a stocky guard more at home on the football field than the hardwood. "They're crazy. They stretch knee ligaments so bad."

He might have been right, but it worked our quads so effectively that we could barely stand up after doing them. My legs felt like Crazy Ikes held together by stretched rubber bands. We finished by running wind sprints right after having done them. Then after the first three "down and backs," when our tongues were touching the floor, Coach Johnson issued a challenge.

"If everyone runs hard you all go in." We ran like kids with our hair on fire and then bending over, grabbing our knees and sucking every last atom of oxygen out of that gym, we heard, "On the line, gentlemen."

My Chuck Taylor All-Stars felt like diver's boots. Trying to inject some humor into the exhaustion, Dwyer lined up next to me, his glasses fogged up and sweat dripping from his chin.

"Oh, feet, don't fail me now," he muttered. On Day #1 even that didn't end the torture. We got to do Killers.

When, mercifully, conditioning was finally done we drug ourselves off the floor and into the showers. Any player who wanted to shoot around after practice wished he hadn't.

"If you're not tired, you didn't work hard enough. Go in," Coach Johnson said. And to make matters worse, the thing was, he'd remember that you weren't tired enough to scramble to the safety of the locker room. That night on the way home on the activity bus Jerry Hollens, our little dead-eye guard, smiled half-heartedly.

"We ran so much stop and go, back and forth, line to line today that my feet felt like they were on fire. I swear, if I would have touched my tennies I'd have burned my fingers."

Sometimes to spice things up on a Friday after our Thursday games, Coach Johnson would arrange with some of his adult buddies to scrimmage our team. Coaches Carlile and Johnson, both college players themselves, would team with Mr. Danielson, the 6'7" journalism teacher. The coach would also invite Mr. Lehl, the athletic 7th grade southpaw coach, Mr. Krebs, a wide body, and the burly Mr. Dove. After our first contest with the adult teachers, Ott arranged for our team to have a little meeting at lunch to plan some strategy for our next encounter. He got an earful, and most of it was complaints about another player, Mr. Keefe.

"All those other guys were nothing compared to Keefe," said Hollens. "He's so hairy and dripped sweat like an overstuffed pig." Leon Keefe, like Mr. Danielson, was tall, maybe 6'4".

"The thing I hate about him," said Ott, "is that he loves to grab your shirt or shorts when you're fighting for a rebound. If you score on him or beat him to a loose ball he will bear hug you and wrestle you to the floor. Then with all his weight pinning you down, he rubs his sweaty iron stubble beard on your face."

At the end of our meeting we all agreed to be more aggressive, especially with Keefe. The next time we scrimmaged we took turns grabbing his shirt and stepping on his feet. We just made sure to run faster and away from him if he swore revenge. The other coaches and adults just laughed at our tactics.

After every league game Coach Johnson handed out a team chart showing stats for the game. Every player's name was listed with columns showing how many rebounds, assists, steals, free throws, each of us got, and what our shooting percentage was. He stressed team play and got after players who jogged over to the scorers' table after a game to ask the scorekeeper how many points they got. He wanted us to remember that the game was about more than points. He praised players for hustle and supporting their teammates. He even had a special award that he pinned up beside the stat sheet on the locker room bulletin board every week. It was a piece of toilet paper with the name of the player who had cast off with the most ridiculous shot during the game. It was called the Crap Shot Award. Show offs got rewarded, too.

All of this paid huge dividends for our team as we made it through the entire season undefeated and, mimicking the Celtics, were declared the league champions that year. A couple of other reasons for our success were the talent of our bench and our starting big guys.

Like Loscutoff our center, Delmar Dykes, was a sort of gentle giant that never really lost his temper. At least, not that we could tell. The absolute worst thing that came out of his mouth was "Oh, phooey." His face might be twisted up in anger or frustration, but his religious upbringing allowed only a limited vocabulary. He was, however, so excited to be playing basket-ball.

"Unlike football (where he was a lineman) I actually get to touch the ball," he joked.

Another wild-eyed player, Mickey "Stretch" Robinson, was blessed with huge hands that once on the basketball floor turned both bright red and ice cold. For some reason, the faster he played, the more this condition increased. All the hot blood seemed to drain from his limbs and recirculate in his core. It was a weird feeling having Mickey pat me on the back in the huddle during timeouts. I wondered if, unlike the rest of us, his feet were also frozen.

That 9th grade basketball season two things happened to me that had never happened before. The first was that I got ejected in the game at Cascade. This was the one school that matched up well with us and the games always seemed to be close.

"Yeah, towards the end of the game they were really in our face trying to catch up. I think we were ahead by a few points when I tried a crossover dribble to get that Conrad guy off me," said Ott. "The dumb ball banged off his knee and one of their guys picked it up and raced down court with the ball. He didn't make the layup," he said with a sort of sadistic grin.

"How could he," laughed Hollens. "He flew right by the backboard and from my viewpoint from behind him I never saw his hands or the ball get above his shoulders. Mark, you rode that mustang right to the wall."

Being the closest player to the driving opponent on the breakaway, I contested the layup. The official called me for shoving him in the back – a flagrant or intentional foul in his opinion – and sent me to the bench. In my mind, there was nothing flagrant about my action. I simply didn't want him to make the basket. If I had intended it to be "flagrant" the wall beyond the basket would have resembled the Wiley Coyote cartoon-like cut out depicting the spot where his body exited the building. I felt it was a homer call, but I plopped down on the bench and said nothing. In the dressing room after the game Coach Johnson came over and put his hand on my shoulder.

"You should go into the coach's office and find the official that made the call. Apologize to him for your "flagrant" foul and tell him you just were trying to prevent a score," he said as a grin crept across his face. I did what he suggested even though I knew I had barely touched the flopping Cascade player. We won the game and I moved on.

The other was thing that happened that season was being a part of a perfectly executed play just as it had been drawn up. I felt like one of my Celtics swishing a basket in Boston Garden. I heard the roar of the crowd just as if I had been Jim Luscatoff setting the backboard pipes back in place.

For a home game against Thurston, Coach Johnson, ever the innovator, drew up a play reminiscent of our "58 Special." Like the football play, this was a designed play for our first offensive possession. I don't recall if it had a name – it probably did – but the results were just the same.

Dykes won the tip, and the ball was brought down into front court by Hollens, the guard on the left side of our 2-1-2 offensive set. Hollens passed to Ott, the other guard on his right, who passed to me on the right wing. Once I received the ball I passed it back to Ott. This was the signal for Stretch, the forward on the other side and Delmar, our center, to set a double screen for me cutting hard across the key to the spot vacated by Stretch. Ott zipped it to Hollens who flung it to me cutting off the double screen. I caught it and twisted to my right for a little two-foot jumper that swished through the net.

In my Boston Garden fantasy I had spun a perfect reverse layup off the backboard like Bob Cousy. In the real world of the Hamlin gym that afternoon I made the only shot I felt comfortable in trying, a short twisting jumper. This play succeeded because of two things that I loved about basketball, timing and teamwork. Having completed the play just as it was designed to be run, I raced back down court. I could see the smiles from my teammates and hear the cheering of my peers in the crowd. Dad was in the stands watching and so was Emily Vinson. My chest puffed out and my feet felt as light as feathers. I was so proud to be a Celtic Logger.

I remember the good feeling that came with the winning, but what I value more is what I learned under my basketball coaches at Hamlin: the correct fundamentals they stressed and insisted on. To this day it frustrates me to see college and professional players still making the stupid mistakes that should have been corrected when they were first learning the game. Under coaches Carlile and Johnson we had several rules that were carved in stone like the Ten Commandments. When I coached basketball with young players in elementary or middle school years later I repeated the mantras:

1. No opponent should beat you on the baseline. When guarding an opponent in that area you are to put one foot on the baseline – straddle it Coach Johnson insisted – to force your opponent either out of bounds or back into the help of your teammates.

2. *Don't reach. When guarding a dribbling opponent, play defense with your feet. It's all about position. This rule got screamed from the coaches in practice. And a little addition to this rule that was one I have never heard from any coaches anywhere since: Turn your palms up when you poke at a dribble. Never swat down; the refs will always call that. When you swipe up you will most likely contact the ball and knock it into their legs creating a turnover for your team.*

3. *On offense, always pass to your teammate's outside hand. I think it is interesting that Oregon's new coach, Dana Altman, also insists on this skill.*

4. *After we scored or after a turnover, always beat your opponent down the floor, turn around and be squared up waiting for him. I can remember JC yelling at players regarding this rule. "You can't play defense from the side" (on an opponent driving down the floor).*

5. *When you rebound, put your opponent on your back. With your knees bent to leap for the ball you should have your palms turned back by your hips to "feel" your opponent and slide with him.*

6. *When being screened by the opposing team, always try to fight over the screen first.*

SMALL 10-12

Butterick

9981
50c

QUICK 'N EASY

Devil or Angel?

"Devil or angel, I can't make up my mind.
Which one you are..."
Bobby Vee

Although the girls might not have understood the intrica-cies of the sports world, one of the things they were defi-nitely focused on was how they dressed. They knew how to attract attention, the boys' attention especially, just by what they wore.

"You know, before every social gathering we planned ex-actly what we were going to wear down to the very last detail," said Annette. That became blatantly obvious when Annette, Emily, and Suzanne Jeffries all showed up for a late spring party one night in Bermuda shorts and angel blouses. These blouses were lightweight white cotton with scooped necks and short, off-the-shoulder angel sleeves. The necklines, sleeve ends, and the bottoms of the blouse were embellished with embroidery. The risqué part was that the bottom of the blouse hung just below the wearer's rib cage. This left skin showing.

Guys' imaginations had a field day, especially Earl's. Pepsi in hand he strolled over next to me and leaned in close to my ear.

"If that isn't a come on, Mark, I don't know what is," he said his eyes locked in on Annette's belly button. I'm not complaining, mind you, but it's killing me to stand here and look." Just then Connie Byers, who was hosting the party, slipped on a slow song, *Teen Angel,* and Earl bee-lined across Connie's square-tiled family room floor. He grabbed Annette and, as they faced one another, slid his right hand around to her lower back. Skin settled on skin. He pulled her in close. Meanwhile Bruce and I, pretending to be casually discussing the potential of this year's mosquito crop, were giving each other play-by-play updates on Earl's maneuvers.

"His thumb is now hidden by the bottom of her blouse, but I can still see a wrist," Bruce reported. My back was to the dancers, but I was already busy memorizing Suzanne's outfit at the snack table. Bruce continued. "I don't want to keep staring. Check that. I do, but you need to take a turn while I enjoy the view from the potato chip bowl. I don't want it to be so obvious. Not that it isn't already."

"Oh, boy," I said being tagged to continue the reporting. "Now Earl's wrenched her in tighter. He's gripping her kidney. Her eyes are closed and she's smiling! Let's get some fresh air. It's getting hot in here." As we headed to the screen door the song ended. A horde of girls raced behind us to the bathroom just down the hall. Jerry Hollens and a grinning Earl followed Bruce and me outside.

"I'm telling you," Earl began. "Those blouses are NICE! You can just sit there and drool like you have been, or you can suck it up and go have some fun. You know you want to. And they want you to. Why do you think they wore them in the first place?"

After a brief cool off Earl's challenge fueled our return to the family room. The party continued. About half an hour later Connie brought out some home made pizza and we all began joking and unwinding from the first couple hours' social niceties. When all the pizza had disappeared Connie put on some music and Bruce and I helped clean up. The night was pleasantly warm, and before long it got a bit warmer. Following Earl's needling, I found myself dancing to almost every 45 Connie put on. My favorites were the slow dances with Emily. Just as the party was sorting itself out into its inevitable pairings, Connie burst into the room.

"Oh, God, my brother's home. You guys need to leave right now. If my parents find out I've had this party I'll be in a lot of trouble. I'll call you all tomorrow. Now go!" It was then that I realized I hadn't seen Connie's parents around that night.

Quickly we grabbed out coats and hurried out the screened rear door into the back yard and then onto railroad tracks beyond. We scattered. Bruce, Suzanne, and Jerry turned left and headed for Bruce's house in town; I grabbed Emily's hand and turned right. Earl grabbed Annette's and followed.

"My house is just a couple blocks away," I said. "We'll be there in a few minutes. You can call your folks and tell them to pick you up there rather than Connie's. We'll think of some excuse for the change." The short hike took longer that I predicted, however. Earl and AJ bolted ahead inventing some game about leaping from railroad tie to railroad tie. Before long they were barely visible in the darkening night. Emily and I watched their playfulness for a while. Then, rooted firmly to the gravel beneath our feet, we began a game of our own choosing. Ten minutes later we caught up with our friends and slid through the blackberry bushes and across the barbwire fence into my back yard. Parents were phoned. AJ talked her folks into letting her stay overnight at Emily's; Earl had already arranged to stay the night with me.

The next morning while we were eating breakfast the phone rang. It was Bruce.

"Hey, Mark, you got a minute? I think you'll want to hear this. I guess the phone lines have been hot this morning. In fact, I got a midnight call from Suzanne and we talked for almost an hour nonstop.

"Wait a sec, Bruce. I'm going to drag this phone into the bedroom." I excused myself from the table and motioned for Earl to follow me. We put the phone up between our heads so we both could hear.

"OK, go ahead," I said.

"You remember that girls' stampede to the bathroom last night after Earl and AJ's *Teen Angel* dance? Well, I guess once they all got in the bathroom AJ went on and on about what it felt like feeling Earl's hands on her bare back. There was quite a commotion and lots of questions and giggling. At least that's what Suzanne said. She said that AJ got all the girls curious and wanting to see for themselves what it was like."

"Yeah, when we came back in from the back yard things seemed to be a bit different," I said. "Jerry and Suzanne seemed to be enjoying each other's company a lot the remainder of the party. Did Suzanne say anything else?"

"You might find Emily's reaction interesting," Bruce teased. "She said that she and AJ and Suzanne had seen the blouses in Eugene while shopping a couple of weeks ago and thought they were pretty wild. On a dare they each bought one and decided to try it out at a party. They wanted guys, certain guys specifically, to notice them, to pay attention to them. They weren't sure what reaction they'd cause if you can believe that. All the other girls in the bathroom were asking how much they cost and where they got them. We may be seeing a lot more of them based on everyone's reaction."

"Hey, Bruce," Earl said grabbing the phone out of my hand. "You can't tell me they didn't know what reaction those little angel blouses would have on us guys. They wanted to get our attention, huh. Well, they sure got mine. On the tracks on the way to Mark's house I had some moments that were what every guy dreams of in their favorite fantasies." He handed me the phone back.

"I guess part of the concern from the girls in the bathroom," Bruce continued, "was that maybe not all of them felt they could wear them. But Arlene, never afraid to push the limits, spoke up saying that anyone could look good in them if they had access to enough Kleenex. That got quite a laugh, I guess. She can be pretty blunt at times."

Having heard Bruce's last comments Earl moved close to the phone and blurted, "Well, I can't speak for the rest of the girls, but I'm almost certain AJ doesn't use any Kleenex. Maybe I'll ask Jerry tomorrow about Suzanne."

"Hey, look, I better get off now or Dad will come and yank the cord out. I'll call you back a little later. In the meantime, you might be thinking of what Settlemeyer or Godwin, those two perky flute players in band you keep telling me about, might do to one of those blouses. Oops, I can hear Dad coming. Gotta go. I'll call you later.

Goats

"Holy moly," mumbled the shopkeeper as he shuffled over to the cash register. "I never thought I'd sell that thing in a million years!"

"Well, it's just perfect. How much do I owe you?" Mom had just purchased a plastic Picasso goat about the size of the Michener paperback wedged into a side pocket of her navy blue purse. It had "spoken to her" she said from the dusty shelf in the Newport Lions Club thrift store. With my brother and sister and me in tow she had been poking around in the shops near the charter fishing boat docks, just killing time waiting for Dad to come back from his morning fishing trip. She glanced again at the little goat in the paper bag and again at the three pre-school children she had brought with her into the shop. She couldn't wait to line the kids up and take a picture of them holding that goat. What a chuckle the Belionis would have.

It was only last year that Mrs. Belioni, a fellow Army wife, had cut out a story in the *Saturday Evening Post* and sent it to Mom. It was about two types of offspring that families produced. According to the article all children could either be classed as "sheep" or "goats." Sheep were the nice, polite, correct children most parents hope to raise. Goats were the difficult, contentious, rule-breakers that often achieve fame and notoriety. Mom had decided early on that although she had tried to raise them as sheep, her two boys were definitely goats. Trouble was that she wasn't sure that either would be famous or patent a world cure for anything. She had noticed, however, that both were attracted to challenges and at times could certainly be contentious.

One afternoon in the winter of my 9th grade year I flirted with that belief that Mom had for me being a goat. I had made the basketball team and we were playing Cascade Junior High at home in the Hamlin gym. As was true of almost every game with them, this one was very close, never more than 5 points separating the two teams for the entire game. With 22 seconds to go in the 4th quarter we had the ball but were down by a point. Coach Johnson signaled for a time out to plan a last second strategy. During the break Coach Johnson drew up a play, a simple pick and roll involving our two best shooters, Jerry Hollens and Butch Cluff. He scanned our faces.

"You all understand what we're doing?" he asked. "Any questions? " We looked at each other, a nervous smile erupting on Cluff's face

"Let's kill 'em," he growled. Hollens, his usual poker face plastered on, was all business. No emotion registered for anyone to see. He scanned the rest of the faces in the huddle, one at a time.

"OK, hands in," ordered Coach Johnson. "On three. One-two-three."

"Let's go!" we all yelled.

The referee blew his whistle and waved us out onto the court. He handed me the ball and I flipped it in to Hollens. Everything started just as it should have. Taking my pass Hollens slid to the top of the key following the coach's orders and tried to snap the ball to Cluff to begin the designed play. Following their coach's strategy, the two Cascade guards ran toward Jerry hoping to double team him and cause a tie up or turn over. Sensing what was coming Jerry frantically flipped the ball to me near the right sideline. I glanced at the scoreboard and saw that only 12 seconds remained on the clock. With all the spectators screaming I drove hard to my left toward the basket. As I neared the key the big blond Cascade center swiped at the ball, lost his balance a bit, and bumped into me. The referee blew his whistle. I was headed to the free throw line for a one and one; if I made the first shot I would get a second. Eight seconds remained in the game.

Coach Johnson called time out again. We trotted over to the sideline. He smiled and tried cracking a joke to set me at ease. My teammates patted me on the back and offered encouragement. Then the horn sounded calling us out to the floor. Players lined up in their places along the foul lane. The official bounced me the ball. Clutching the ball in my damp hands, I toed the line, took a deep breath, bent my knees, and eased the ball up toward the basket. It hit the front rim, bounded up, hit the back rim, and rolled in. Pandemonium ensued and with the score now knotted at 41-41, Coach Johnson called our final time out. No one was more relieved than I was. After all, I was only a 67% free throw shooter that season, meaning that I would probably make about 6 out of every 10 free throws I attempted.

I had one more coming, but I was pushing the odds if I expected to make the next one.

Probably having calculated those odds way ahead of me, Coach Johnson told me to shoot the ball hard – essentially telling me to miss intentionally – and told my teammates to crash the boards for the rebound. His hope, no doubt, was for us to retrieve the errant free throw for a final shot at the basket or perhaps another free throw line opportunity for someone else on my team, someone who was a better free throw shooter. When he had finished his instructions he looked right at me.

"Mark, do you understand? Shoot it hard for the back rim." I heard his words, but my brain was having difficulty processing what he had just asked me to do. I just nodded.

The horn sounded and we hustled out to our places along the free throw lane once again. All the cheering and yelling stopped. Total silence. My teammates leaned in against the Cascade players on the lane like an accordion being squeezed together for the final note, everyone poised for the rebound. The referee again bounced me the ball and held up an index finger.

"One shot. Play it if he misses," he barked. Again I wiggled my right foot and inched up to the line, took a deep breath, and eyed the basket. A nagging thought kept elbowing its way toward the front of my brain disrupting my concentration. How do I successfully miss this shot? I never tried to intentionally miss a shot before. I didn't have to. I usually did that all by myself automatically four times out of every ten at the line. In all the excitement I must have misunderstood Coach Johnson, I thought. Aw heck, I'm just going to shoot it like I always do. Well, maybe not like always. I took a deep breath, exhaled and released the ball in a slow backspin. All the eyes that I could feel pressing against me as I stood at the line slid off me and onto the spinning ball as it arced up and then began its descent toward the hoop. Instead of the coach's desired clang off the orange back rim or white metal backboard, there was no sound. Just the barely audible swish as the ball fell cleanly through the net and hit the parquet floor. Then the roar and screams of the crowd blew silence out the doors.

The Cascade guard, "Tweety" we called him because of the reddish hair on his head combed back in a little DA, grabbed the ball, stepped out of bounds, and frantically looked for a teammate to inbound it to. Players were running all over the court waving their arms, coaches were yelling, spectators screaming. It felt like being inside a guitar at a Ventures concert. With precious seconds ticking off the scoreboard clock Tweety fired the ball towards the sideline to a teammate. The Cascade player leaped up to catch it, but the ball slid off his outstretched fingertips and into the crowd as the buzzer sounded and time expired.

We had won a thriller, 42-41. I got the congratulatory hugs and backslapping on the court with my teammates as we all trotted over to the bench. Coach Johnson pulled me aside.

"Purdue, that effort at the line deserves a milkshake. I owe you."

I never did get the milkshake. But then, being honest with myself, I had to admit that I hadn't exactly followed Coach Johnson's instructions. As I unlaced my Chuck Taylor All Stars in the dressing room after the game I wondered if that Picasso goat sitting on the mantel above the fireplace at home would be grinning. No, probably not. That would be Mom when Dad told her about the game. And what Coach Johnson had told me to do. And what I did.

Girls Just Wanna Have Fun

Numerous attempts to break the laws that parents set came into play during these junior high days. Sneaking out at night to meet up with a few others who had tried to do the same was one. Girls' slumber parties or overnighters at friends' houses usually provided the perfect opportunity.

Annette Jensen, or AJ as we frequently called her, had arranged with her parents to stay overnight at Emily Vinson's house after a Friday night Teen Canteen dance at the Memorial Building. They had planned to meet Stephanie, a classmate, later that night near the big ditch on the north side of Willamalane Park.

When they got home from the dance AJ and Emily stayed up watching TV for a while, then wished the elder Vinsons goodnight and headed into Emily's bedroom. Before long Emily's parents clicked off the set, projected their good nights down the hallway, and padded off to bed as well. Emily switched off her bedroom light. The two girls lay on Emily's bed whispering for almost half an hour. When Emily thought her parents had gone to sleep and it was safe, she slowly raised the bedroom window. She stuck her right leg out and straddled the sill. AJ helped push Emily's head down to clear the bottom of the window. Then, grabbing hold of her left foot so she wouldn't fall, AJ eased Emily out. Emily slid quietly down into the flowerbed.

AJ was about six inches taller and couldn't scissor her way out like Emily had done. She turned over on her stomach and, using the dresser chair, stuck both her feet out the window while pushing up against the chair cushion with her arms. With her stomach resting on the sill, her stiffened body balanced like a teeter totter board on a fulcrum. As she dropped her feet to the ground the back of her head smacked the bottom of the window.

"Oh, ouch," AJ groaned. Then she began to laugh.

"Shhh," Emily whispered while crumpling to the lawn, her hands covering her mouth in an attempt to muffle her own laughter. Finally getting control of themselves, the two slinked around the side of the house. They were just about to the driveway and on their way when Mrs. Vinson suddenly materialized on the sidewalk ten feet to the left. Unbeknownst to Emily, her mom had decided to go next door to visit a neighbor instead of turning in with Mr, Vinson.

"Emily, what are you doing out?

"Oh, nothing," she said. "AJ and I had a bet. She bet me she could find the Big Dipper. We were looking for it."

"Well, you better come in now." Reluctantly the twosome followed her into the house.

"Geez, AJ" Emily whispered once inside the safety of her bedroom. "What were we thinking?" Then she began to giggle.

AJ, catching the infectious sound, buried her head in a pillow to stifle her laughter.

"Wonder what Stephanie's thinking right about now?" mused Emily out loud. "I'll have to call her early tomorrow morning and explain."

"Yeah, we were pretty stupid," said AJ, "but I loved the excitement. So much fun. My head may have a different opinion, however."

About a half a mile away another group of Springfield Jr. High girls tried their luck one night during an outside summer sleepover in Lindsay Snyder's back yard. Lindsay's parents were a little more lax about keeping an eye on things. When Lindsay saw the light go out in her parents' bedroom she waited, giving them time to fall asleep. Even though there was lots of talking and laughing in the back yard, the elder Snyders, despite the ruckus, nodded off.

"Oh, you guys. Let's do something wild and exciting," suggested a hyped-up Gina Wittingham. "How about we sneak by Gary's house, see if there are any lights still on, or if maybe we can catch a glimpse of him in the window."

"He's so cute!" moaned Jessie.

That's all it took. With Gina in the lead the pack of girls exited the back yard. Keeping to the shadows, in a short time found themselves approaching Gary Nelson's house. As they drew near, the small group bunched up at the front of a long six-foot laurel hedge that divided the Nelson's property from their neighbors to the east. Lights were on in the Nelson's house, but all the shades were drawn.

"Shoot, not much to look at here," said Jessie.

"Maybe I can fix that," said Gina. Leaping the low white picket fence, Gina softly sprinted along the laurel hedge till she got even with the Nelson's front flowerbed. Then dropping to her hands and knees, she crawled across the front yard and under the front window till she reached the small cement porch. Extending into a crouch she turned and flashed a huge Cheshire grin to her small group of friends on the sidewalk. Turning back towards the porch, she reached out and punched the doorbell three times, then bolted across the front of the house and slipped herself inside the leafy hedge. After about 15 long seconds the front porch light flipped on and Mr. Nelson stepped out. He surveyed the dark yard. Gary pushed open the screen door and stuck his head out.

"Who was it?" Gary asked.

"Beats me. Probably some of your smart aleck friends for all I know." Both Nelsons stepped back in the house, Mr. Nelson closing the door behind him. When she thought it was safe to crawl out of the hedge Gina, keeping one eye on the house, slipped back to her group.

"How's that for you, Jessie?" beamed Gina.

"You're crazy, but that's what we love about you. Now how about we see what's happening at Derek's. It's just a few blocks from here."

"Lead the way, Jessie." I'm right behind you."

"And what about you Jackie?" teased Tonya. "Wouldn't you like to grab a glimpse of Lonnie? You know, something to take to your pillow tonight?" She giggled.

"What's so funny?" said Jackie joining the laughter.

"Oh, nothing. I was just admiring that pretty candy-cane striped sunburn on your left calf. That's what you get for falling asleep in your back yard getting a suntan. Bet you don't cross your legs next time."

"Shut up, Gina." Then unable to keep a serious face, Jackie burst out laughing.

"Hey, don't you think sneaking around at night peeking at boyfriends' houses is fun? Ah, what a riot," said Gina.

Speaking of a riot," said Lindsay, "remember that time during a sleepover at Jessie's? While her parents were out, a group of us decided to call a fraternity at the U of O as a prank. The conversation kept getting bolder. We pretended to be lonely, curious high school seniors. The next thing we knew there was a knock on the door. Some of us were scared to death, but Gina and Jessie casually stepped to the door and opened it. You can only imagine the looks on the frat boys' faces to see 14-year-old girls giggling. Not what they were hoping for, I'm sure."

"Geez, how we laughed and carried on after they left," said Tonya. "That next week every time the phone rang at night I worried it might be those frat guys wanting to talk to my parents. I had nightmares about it."

A Kiss is Just a Kiss?

"You must remember this, a kiss is just a kiss,
A sigh is just a sigh..."
"As Time Goes By" (Herman Hupfeld, 1931T)

For all of us guys entering adolescence, lip-to-lip contact with a girl proved to be an interesting experiment, to say the least. How did one go about it? What would it feel like? This kind of experimentation was not like science class! I kept thinking about how I felt during my on-the-job training, that scary moment at the beginning of my 8th grade year in the Arts and Crafts room alcove with Ronnie. For me it always felt like walking out to the end of the high dive for the first time, staring down at the water three miles below, and knowing I was just supposed to jump.

From the parties I was invited to that first junior high year, I was regaled with stories of those initial party kisses. The metallic bump of braces mixed with the tang of barbecue potato chips. Different scents of perfume, the taste of lipstick. Crushing kisses. Gentle teasing kisses. The moist warm breath expelled through a girl's nose. *In a lengthy liplock all breathing was done through our noses.* As guys, most of us just practiced what we'd seen in the movies and then compared notes later. For others the experiences may have been different, but they were never forgotten.

"My first kiss was with Rich," said Erin, a tall freckle-faced tomboy. "It seemed so sloppy. Lots of slobber. I didn't like it at all." But for her things improved with practice as she acquired more boyfriends.

One Saturday afternoon Gary, her boyfriend at the time, asked her if she'd like to go to the movies. His parents dropped them off at the McKenzie Theater on Main Street. They paid their $.50 admission, grabbed some popcorn and Cokes at the counter, then parted the velvet burgundy curtains separating the lobby from the theater seats and settled into the very back row. Before long they had nervously devoured all the popcorn and set what remained of their Cokes on the floor by their feet. Erin felt Gary's right arm hesitantly slide over the back of her seat and come to rest on her shoulders.

Erin kept glancing out of the corner of her eye, but nothing happened. It wasn't until after the newsreel and comics had finished and the first feature began that Gary swiveled his head around for a kiss. As Erin twisted to meet his lips she knocked over her Coke. The syrupy liquid trickled down the cement-sloped floor under the rows in front of them.

Erin and Gary made out off and on throughout the double feature. After the movie was over they stumbled outside into the sunlight to meet his folks who were picking them up. As soon as she got home Erin immediately called Emily for a report.

"The movie date with Gary was so much fun. I can still smell the buttery popcorn on his breath." Emily just listened as Erin rattled on. "You know, I had always wondered what it would be like to kiss him. When his folks picked us up our faces were all red and scratchy. I'm sure they didn't have a clue what we had been doing."

Dave Williams, another one of us great pretenders, began his kissing apprenticeship in 6th grade with Spin-the-Bottle and Post Office games at friends' parties. It was usually just a quick peck followed by blushing and giggles. A couple years later, however, Dave got "schooled" by a clarinet player.

"My 9th grade year when I was in the band I had a huge crush on a girl named Sammi French from one of the other junior highs in town. She was beautiful with dark brown eyes, full lips, and quite a mature body compared to the other girls our age.

"After rehearsal one night I offered her a ride home. Mom drove. I walked her up the driveway and around the corner of her house to her front porch. She turned to face me. Our eyes locked." *Yikes, now what?*

Throwing caution to the wind Dave zeroed in on those lips, closed his eyes and arched his neck forward. Taking the cue, Sammi rocked up on her toes towards him. As their lips met her mouth opened slightly.

"HER TONGUE TOUCHED MINE," he said. "Underneath my closed lids my eyes snapped to the bridge of my nose, chills crawled up my back, and beads of perspiration formed on my forehead. She then proceeded to move her tongue around exploring mine. After making sure I was sufficiently confused and aroused, she ended the kiss, turned, and opened the front door."

"Good night," she said, a wry smile stamped on her face.

"She knew what she had done," said Dave. With my head still spinning I tugged my sweater down low to cover the bulge in my cords and stumbled like a drunk to the car. *You've got to watch those preacher's daughters.* Apparently, the sweat on my forehead and my thousand-yard stare prompted my mom to ask if I was OK.

"Yeah," I replied with my voice cracking. "I'm fine." But she knew I wasn't.

"I'm not sure if my mom said anything else to me on the way home," Dave told me. "All I could think about was calling my best friend to tell him what had just happened. I was sure I had just had sex, or something like it because it felt so good. I could hardly wait to do it again. I was convinced Sammi was in love with me. After all, we had just had…well, whatever it was."

Photo Credits

Hamlin Junior High Sketch (cover, verso page, story title pages) courtesy of Springfield School District Administration office... artist unknown

Washburn Historic District house...author photo

1953 Chevrolet sedan...(www.53classicchevy.com), page 0

Levi's newspaper ad...(www.pinterest.com), page 6

School bus...(www.mccleanbus.com/school-bus), page 8

Saul T. Rose and teachers...Hamlin Jr. High *Wedge*, 1960, page 22

Ricky Nelson album cover...(www.rockabillyhall.com/rickynelson), page 32

Riddell shoes...(www.sportsmemorabiliamuseum.com), page 40

Wrestling photo...Hamlin Jr. High *Wedge*, 1960, page 44

8th Grade Basketball picture...Hamlin Jr. High *Wedge* 1960, page 48

Beanpicker...(www.pinterest.com), page 54

Alexander's advertisement...*Springfield News* microfilm at Knight
Library, August 1960, page 62

Party invitation...Randy Bryson personal memorabilia, page 74

Bicycle ad...(flickrhivemind.net), page 88

Junior State Baseball team...Kirk Kneeland personal photo, page 96

1950 Ford newspaper ad...(www.pinterest.com), page 102

Willamalane Swimming Pool photos...courtesy of City of
Springfield and Willamalane Park and Recreation, pages 116, 198

9th Grade Football picture...Hamlin Jr. High *Wedge*, 1961, page 128

Premier drum...(marching.premier-percussion.com), page 132

Movie ad...microfilm of *Springfield News*, July 1960, page 146

Olympia beer bottle...(enjoyolympiabeer.com), 156

Angel Baby 45 rpm record...(www.acerecords.co.uk/angel-
babyrevisited), page 162

9th Grade Basketball picture...Hamlin Jr. High *Wedge*, 1961, page
176

Butterick pattern #9981...(www.pinterest.com), page 186

Picasso Goat...Kirk Kneeland memorabilia, page 192

McKenzie Theater photo courtesy of Springfield Historic Museum,
page 204

Mid-1950s Springfield

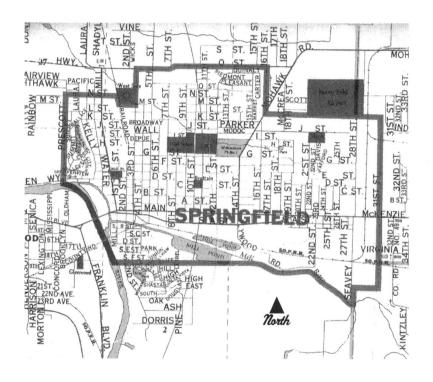

Main Street Springfield, 1958

	Mill Street
151 Orchard Auto Parts	112 Dunnington Service Station
	152 Hal Bryan Service Station

	2nd Street
215 Timber Topper	204 Sasser's Spfld. Cleaners
225 Spfld. Glass	208 Fitch-Huggins Insurance
229 Brandt Finance	228 Masonic Temple
255 Bud's Union Station	240 Star Café
	244 Wilson's Barber Shop

	3rd Street
303 The Corral	326 Turner's Hardware & Paint
307 Valley Hotel	Western Union
311 Harkins Flooring	Spfld. Sheet Metal
321 Vern Allen Real Est.	330 Hansen Furniture
323 House of Lights	336 apartments
325 Les Pruit's Barber	342 Spfld. IOOF
327 State Farm Ins.	346 SUB
331 Light's for Music	350 The Beauty Spot
339 Daniel's Barber	
341 Rainbow Café	
349 Spfld. Flowers	4th Street

	4th Street
403 St. Vincent de Paul	412 Spfld. Chamber of Commerce
407 Stone's Men's Wear	414 Gas Lamp Tavern & Restaurant
415 The Club	420 Pimentel Electric
423 Coast to Coast Stores	428 ½ Dee & Bob's Barber Shop
439 Spfld. Furniture Co.	434 The Spar Tavern
445 Ed Harms, Attny.	442 Oregon Outfitters
449 U.S. National Bank	444 Rolling Pin Bakery
	448 Oldfield's Electric

MAIN STREET

Main Street Springfield, 1958

5th Street

503 Burge Firestone	500 Gerlach's Drug Store
515 Walt Laxton's Store for Men	516 Wright's Hardware & Furniture
519 Adair Shop	538 Alexander's Dept. Store
521 Moderne Photo (Light's in 1964)	550 Pacific Power & Light
525 Hull's Café	
535 Fort & Co. (later Kaufman Bros.)	
553 Willamette Press & Stationery	
555 Hill's Jewelers	

6th Street

Springfield News	602 Springfield Pharmacy
611 U.S. Post Office	612 F.W. Woolworth & Co.
615 McElhany Shoe Repair	630 McKenzie Theater
637 Fee & Ritchey Jewelers	640 Iverson's Paints
639 Spfld. Health Foods	650 88 Cents Store
641 E. Zimmerman Real Estate	660 City Center Super Market
(Equitable Savings & Loan)	
643 Spfld. Stationery	
647 Jack Frost Shoe Repair	

MAIN STREET

7th Street

First National Bank	700 Leather's Richfield (1958)
713 Varsity Theater (1958)	742 Spfld. Insurance Agency
715 Spfld. College of Beauty	750 John's Mobil Station
725 Home Finance	
Spfld. Elks Lodge	
731 Hamlin-Shockley Real Estate	
737 Texas Hot Dog	

8th Street

John Brown's Service Station	816 Vitus Service Station
831 Hart Dairy Queen	844 Main Motel
853 S & L Motors	868 Spfld. Auto Parts (1964)

9th Street

	Parchen Shell Service Station
	914 C & J Tire Company
	924 Timber Bowl
	960 Russ's Union Station

10th Street

Made in the USA
Lexington, KY
01 March 2016